I'M BLIND...
What's Your Excuse?

*A Testimony of How in Our Weakness,
Christ is Made Strong*

DR. RON LESTER

PRESS

Printed in the United States of America

ISBN 9781629525631

Scripture quotations taken from the Holy Bible, New International Version, Copyright © 1973, 1978, 1984 by International Bible Society.

www.xulonpress.com

ACKNOWLEDGMENTS

To Pastor Wayne Thompson, who encouraged me to go into the full time ministry; Pastor David Earls, for the information about Route 13; Pastor Dale Gentry, for the Forward; and all those who encouraged me to complete this book. Thank you.

ACKNOWLEDGMENTS

DEDICATION

———⟨∞⟩———

I am dedicating this book to my wife, Betty, who has stayed with me now for forty-seven years and has lived this book, and to my sons, Rob and James, whom I have called upon many times for help.

This is a short statement about my eyes: I did not know I had a problem with my eyes until I got back from Vietnam in '67. For a good part of my early life, I just thought I had poor eyesight and needed glasses.

So you have a problem. You may be broken. You may have a physical ailment. This is not the end of the world. Get up and do something. You can do it!

TABLE OF CONTENTS

———∞∞∞———

FOREWORD

⸺∞⸺

In all of my forty-seven years of ministry, I have never met a man more diligent, determined, and faithful than Ron Lester. I have known Ron since August 1979, when he came to serve as my assistant at the church I was pastoring in Del City, a suburb of Oklahoma City.

He and his wife Betty were wonderful to work with and became close friends with my wife, Jean, and I. Ron and Betty stood with us through thick and thin, were loyal and very committed to their assignments.

Even though Ron had a seeing disorder, from the time he came to work with us, he never complained or used his handicap as an excuse. In fact, we didn't even know that Ron was legally blind for several years. If I had known, I would never have asked him to drive two hundred miles en route to a conference in Davenport, Iowa. In the middle of the night, Jean and I decided to catch a nap and commissioned Ron to take the wheel. We found out later that his wife Betty sat next to him saying in a quiet voice, "Left, Ron, left, right, Ron, right," instructing him each mile of the way until we finally woke up and stopped for breakfast. Ron didn't want us to know that he was legally blind because he wanted to make sure that he was an asset and not a liability. He was determined from the outset of his seeing disability that he was not going to allow his blindness to prevent him from accomplishing all that was in his heart to do. What an amazing man!

I have followed Ron's journey for the past thirty-something years and have been overwhelmed by the tremendous progress he has made during his lifetime. He overcame difficult circumstances as a boy, served in Vietnam, pastored a church in the desert, led a church in a very dangerous area of Los Angeles, gave oversight to a Christian school, became a successful businessman as well as a motivational speaker, and earned a doctorate degree! I am so honored to have Ron Lester in my life and so thankful to have the opportunity to recommend this book to everyone. Along the way, Dr. Lester has disregarded every opportunity to live on his disability check and listen to television all day. He has approached life with a smile, a vision, a wonderful attitude, and a mountain of faith. This is a great book for everyone to read, particularly those who feel they are limited in life. Read Ron's story and then pass it along. Someday a movie will be made from this book.

Dale Gentry
Breakout Prayer Network
Austin, Texas

Chapter 1

EARLY LIFE

I n 1948, the farmhouse we were renting near Purcell, Oklahoma, was blown away by a twister. We had just come back from church. My family was late getting back because it had been raining and the roads were very muddy. Dad had to back up the big hill by our house, and this had further delayed us. The car's headlights were shining on the front of the house as my parents talked about who should go in to turn on some lights while the other got the babies out of the car. All of a sudden, it got real still. Dad and Mom looked at each other, and then jumped back in the car. Then it hit.

The twister hit the house, which just seemed to vanish, leaving all the furniture exposed. In the next few seconds, everything else was scooped up and carried away. Pots and pans hit the right door of the car so hard that Mom couldn't get it open. They decided to drive down the road to where my Uncle Carl, Dad's brother, lived to see if they had any damage. Uncle Carl's family had been sound asleep and did not know anything had happened.

The Red Cross moved us into a little house that had no insulation and no inside walls. Mom and Dad nailed feed sacks up on the inside to help keep the wind out. We got one of those potbelly wood stoves, and we cooked on it. When the wind would start to blow from the north, you would freeze on one side and burn up on the other. That old place was not much. Dad and Mom hardly had two nickels to rub together.

In 1949, Dad accepted a sharecropping job on a farm in Rosedale, Oklahoma. He was paid $150 per month, an end-of-year share of the crops, and an annual cow and two pigs for butchering. At the time, this was a great deal, but it was a lot of work. The farm covered about four hundred acres and had not been farmed for many years. The grass was so tall, you had to stand on the seat of the tractor to see where you were going. To solve the problem, we burned off the whole place so we could see what was there.

There were no fences or markers to show where any fields should be.

The first thing Dad did was fence the whole place. Then he fenced off a section for farming and other parts for pastures. We had this one area at the bottom of our land with a spring running right down the middle of the field. Dad built a big pond area to hold the water back until he got it seeded. But in no time, that spring of water had filled the pond and was running over. Dad worked from daylight to dark.

The next thing Dad had to get done was to build a milk barn. Several neighbors helped. In those days, everybody helped each other without getting paid because they knew they would be calling on you for help next week or next month. After we got that building done, they built a big, round hay barn with an opening on the east side for feeding the cows in the winter.

The first cows we got were some milk cows. At the beginning, we did not have any power on the property, and for a while Dad would use the tractor for the milking. He would hook up a belt to a generator, and this way he could get the cows milked. We had to use this system many times when the power went out. That was the first time I saw running water and lights.

Many times, I had to clean out the milk barn after the milking was done. I hosed it down and put lime around to dry it up. It always stunk after those cows were milked.

To get water to our home, Dad drove a sand point down about twenty feet, and we got all the water we needed. I remember that in 1956, the drought got so bad that Dad drove the sand point down about ten more feet. Then we got plenty of water.

The old house had two bedrooms, a living room, and a kitchen. It had no running water and no restroom. Instead, it had an old outhouse that was about to fall down. One thing the old house had was a great big basement. It took several months for the electricity company to bring in the necessary electricity poles, so we used cold oil lamps. We moved into the basement while we put a new floor down in the main house.

We had a great big fireplace that you could stand up in—at least, I could back then. The first winter we were there, we built a fire in the fireplace and still froze. We finally got a gas stove to heat the house, but the windows were about to fall out, so we could only heat one room at a time and had to just shut the other rooms off. I remember going to the bedroom, and it was like ice. We had feather mattresses. The nice thing about those mattresses was that we could sink down into them and get warm. Mom would cover us with quilts and then tuck us in so we would be as warm as toast—it was like a good sleeping bag.

My first job was to feed about twelve baby calves on the bucket. This was a hard job for me as a little boy of six years old. I would carry these buckets of milk out to the calves and have to fight the calves back to feed two at a time. Sometimes the calves would fight over the bucket and turn it over and spill it out on the ground. This would make Dad very mad at me.

Dad often liked to use that big old leather belt! I think, nowadays, they would take us kids away because of child abuse. But in those days, we did not think anything about it. It was just a part of growing up.

Chapter 2

LIFE GROWING UP

—⚬⚬⚬—

One of the worst times in my life was when I started to school. We lived about five miles from the town of Rosedale, Oklahoma, and we had a little school there. We had three classrooms. The first, second, and third grades were in one room. Then the fourth, fifth, and sixth grades were together. Then we had seventh and eighth together. Those first few days were bad. I did not want to go to school. I cried and screamed. I ran after Dad. I think this went on for about two weeks.

I don't remember learning anything in the first grade, and I certainly did not learn how to read. The thing that sticks out in my mind was that one day, some of the boys got one of the other boys' caps and started playing keep away. It went flying from one person to another. The cap they were playing with belonged to a friend of mine who was also in the first grade. We were both smaller than the rest of the boys in the class. They were the second and third grade boys. When the teacher saw what was happening, she stopped the boys, but by then the cap was destroyed. She took those boys and stood them at the chalkboard and made them stand on their tiptoes. She then made them stretch as high as they could get their hands to go up and marked where they could reach. Every time they got tired, relaxed, and dropped below that line, she would give them a lick with her board. Every one of the boys got at least three licks. This went on for at least thirty minutes. Those boys never did that again!

The biggest thing I remember is that I did not learn to read in the first grade, but I could beat everyone else in math and counting.

In second and third grades, I learned nothing. I don't even remember reading. When I did, it was bad, and I would get D's. But I would get A's in math.

I never understood why I could not read until I took a college course on disabilities. I learned then that I had dyslexia. I would memorize everything, like my spelling words. I finally understood my frustration in not being able to read and understand the flow of a sentence. It has been said that four out of five boys have some form of dyslexia.

I do remember that once a teacher told me I must be tone deaf, which may have contributed to my ability to hear the sound of a letter. Some letters like "v" and "b" sound the same, and several other letters sound alike to me.

When I was about seven, we went into a store in the small town of Rosedale, which only had two stores, a gas station, a post office, and two churches. That day, Dad allowed me to go into the store with him to get some things. I picked up some candy and put it in my pocket. When we returned to the truck and got in, Dad asked me what I did in the store. I knew better than try to lie, so I showed him the candy. Boy, was he upset! He got his Bible out and went right to the Ten Commandments. He read the one about stealing and, of course, I begin to cry. He tells me that we are going back in there and telling Mr. Russell that I was sorry for stealing his candy. He marched me right back in there and, at the time, that was the hardest thing I had ever done. You know what happened when we got home. That is right: the belt came off, and I got at least five licks.

There was another time in about the fourth grade when I had gone down to Mr. McCall's store with his son. I took one of those candy bars that was five cents and ate it on the way back to the school. I was so miserable for the next few weeks that I was determined to work for some money to pay back that five cents. One day I finally got the five cents and could hardly wait to go down at lunchtime and give it to Mr. McCall. I told him that I stole a candy bar the last time I was in his store and wanted to pay for it. You know, he was so nice to me that he said, "Let's say you just forgot to pay for it." But he did give me a lecture about taking things without paying for them. I do not remember ever taking anything else without paying for it. The Bible says we are all born into sin. We all have a sinful nature until Christ comes into our heart.

I began to understand sentence structure in the fourth grade, when our teacher started teaching us diagramming. This helped my mechanical mind to see how I was supposed to be reading, spelling, and writing sentences. I started making A's and B's in English. That was the first time I thought school was worth going to.

The fourth grade was also when I was introduced to the 4-H Club. I started going to all the judging contests and began to win lots of ribbons. My greatest challenge was when the county agent came down to the farm and asked Dad if he would let me go judge some pigs and maybe become a member of the judging team. Now, this team had three other people on it already, and they were in the sixth grade. They were two years older than I was at that time. They knew what to expect, because they had been doing it for two years already. We did several trips to pig farms, and we would judge these pigs for first, second, third, and fourth places. I recall one instance when the county agent asked me why I graded them like I did. I was so traumatized that I could not even talk, and I began to cry. I really thought I had done something wrong. But I came to find out he thought I had judged them right and nobody else had gotten it right!

We went from there to the judging contest at state level. There our team placed third overall. I placed fourth in the individual group. None of the other team members even placed in the top twenty. This was out of about two hundred teams from around the state.

I knew I had a gift from that time on. I would do my best to beat out all the other kids in school.

I went out for baseball, and I finally talked my dad into buying me a baseball glove. Every time I got a chance, I would get it out and start throwing the ball in the air and catch it. Sometimes, Dad would hit me some fly balls and I learned to catch them. But he saw that sometimes I would lose the ball in the air and would not be able to catch it, because I did not know where it was. At the time, Dad did not think much about it … until about Christmas time, when I got a bow and arrow.

At about this time, I was playing outside in the parking lot after church. We were playing tag, and I was it. Now this was about nine in the evening, and it was very dark in the parking lot. I was running after one of my friends, in and out of cars. He came to a big hay truck and he saw the bed and went left. I did not see that truck bed. I hit the back of that truck and the steel frame around it. I was going full speed; it was just the right size for my mouth. I lost two teeth and broke two other teeth. The front tooth was a permanent tooth and was broken off at an angle. It was always cutting my lip. I broke the bottom tooth halfway off. We did not have the money to fix them, so I stayed that way 'til I came back from Vietnam in '67, when everybody had to go to the dentist. I still have that same cap after forty-some years. After the dentist put it on, he did not like the color and was going to take it off, so he started hitting it with a hammer and some other kind of tool. It would not come off after about three hits. I thought my whole mouth was going to come loose! I told him to just leave it.

Anyway, when I hit that truck, that should have been a sign for Dad and Mom. Then I got the bow and arrow for Christmas. While learning to use the bow, the arrows would go out some distance, and I would walk out and try to find them. I would walk all around the arrows and not find them. I would ask Dad where the arrows were, and he would come out and say, "They are right here!" and point down at them. He would ask if I could see them, and I would say, "No, I could not." Within the next day or two, he took me to the eye doctor and got me some glasses, which really helped me to see. I could now see the board in the classroom!

That spring, I went out for baseball, and the very first time I got up to bat, the pitcher hit me right in the mouth and busted my lip. Blood was running everywhere. The coach took me to the restroom to clean it up somewhat. So, about thirty minutes later, I came back out, and he told me, "You are going to get right back up there and swing at that ball!" Boy, that was fear all over me! I stood there and never hit a thing. When I did make the team, I would be the first or second hitter. The coach said to get as low as you can, and you will walk every time. He wanted base runners, and that was what I did best. I could steal second without a problem.

Sometimes we would have a game at night, and dad only let me go to a night game one time. That night game was under the lights, and I would lose the ball in the lights. The coach would really be upset with me. That was another sign I was losing my night vision, but nobody thought anything about it at that time.

I played left field and second base, and sometimes I would pitch to warm up the catcher. I just could not throw it fast enough to be a good pitcher. I was the smallest boy in my class, but I was very fast. While playing second base, I could field that ball if it came my direction. I only played until the eighth grade, when we moved to Purcell. Dad would not let me go out for any of the sports there. He would tell me I had too much work to do. He was always finding things for me to do.

Most of the time Dad would find some work for me to do. I would drive the pickup real slow while he would throw out the hay for the cows. Sometimes we would have to feed hay to the cows the whole winter because those freezing rains would come and then it would snow on top of that so the cows could not find the grass.

One year we cut the corn down, made silage, and put it in a silo that had been dug out in the hill by the barn. During the winter, we would feed that back to the cows. When we would dig it out, it would be very hot. If it was very cold, we could lay down in that stuff and get warm. It was still green, but the cows loved it.

The summer of '54 was a very dry year, so Dad and the landlord put in an irrigation system. Now, this was a project for everyone. All of us kids would be called upon to help move these long sprinkler systems. This was very hard work, because you would have to walk through the mud, and your shoes would get so big and heavy.

We would run the pump day and night. One day Dad told Mom to have me go put oil in the pump.

Well, that was fine—I had done it several times before. But this day I got on the tractor, which was out in the front yard. It was pretty cold that morning, and the tractor had not been driven yet, so it was very stiff because there was no power steering. The tractor was facing the house and was about a hundred feet from the front porch. I knew that I had to turn it hard to the left, so I let out on the clutch but could not turn it fast enough. The first thing I knew, I had run right over my new bike! I mean, right over the middle, bending the frame and both wheels. I was so upset. I finally got the tractor killed and climbed off the thing and told Mom I was never going to drive that tractor again. It was about a mile down to the pump, and I had to walk all the way. I think I cried the whole way. Dad finally bought me another used bike for ten dollars.

After the drought of '54 to '56 and then the floods of '57, Dad and Mom knew they were not getting ahead and that it was time for them to start making a move to do something different.

Dad went to welding school in Chicago and got certified as a welder. Then we started to raise chickens and sell eggs on an egg route in Oklahoma City. We sold the eggs for fifty cents a dozen.

Up 'til 1957 we had several years of drought, but something happened to the weather. About the first of June, it began to rain buckets. We had a rain gauge that measured five inches. Dad told me to go out and empty the rain gauge after about twenty minutes. At that time, it was running over. I put it back in its place and ran back inside, totally soaked. It stopped raining after forty-five minutes. The rain gauge was at four inches. So, in forty-five minutes, it had rained nine inches! At that time, we lived down by the river called the South Canadian River. The next morning when we woke up, we heard the cows bawling outside and something that sounded like a train roaring down the track. We all ran out to the back porch and looked down. We could not believe our eyes. The river was out of its banks, and all you could see was water for three miles across the whole valley! The two hundred acres of corn that we had planted was washed away.

The rains kept coming, and the river overflowed its banks three times that year. The worst part of it was that the river changed course and started to impact our farm by cutting big blocks of land. It cut about forty acres overnight. Dad and several of the neighbors tried to stop the loss by putting large trees along the banks and tying them with cables to hold them. That would last but a few days and away they would go … right down the river. That year we lost over a hundred acres, plus the irrigation wells.

Chapter 3

WORK ETHIC

––––∞∞∞––––

We did manage to plant some milo in the late summer. We had to wait 'til the ground froze before we could get into the fields to harvest it.

Dad had tried to harvest some of the grain in October and got the tractor and combine stuck in the mud, and he could not get it out 'til the freeze came. So when it froze over, Dad called on my uncle to come over and help. He had an old pickup. So what Dad put him to doing was to shove the grain out of the pickup into a place we called the feed storage. What dad wanted me to do was to drive the pickup behind the combine, and when the bin would get full, pull the pickup up beside the combine and put the grain in the pickup bed. Then I would drive the pickup up the hill to the barn. There my uncle would shovel the grain into the bin. We would trade pickups, and I would drive the one he had just emptied back down the hill. Dad said he would give me a quarter for every load I took up the hill. I made twelve trips up that hill that first day and about ten the next. That was a lot of grain. The cows would not eat it until we ground it up and put some molasses in it to make it sweet, but the pigs would eat it just fine. It was almost as good as corn. That year, we had many geese stop in the field and take a few days to eat what grain was left.

The one thing that was a real blessing that year was that we had over three hundred pecan trees in the bottom. That year we harvested pecans like never before. The years before, there was nothing from those trees. Pecans love lots of water in May and June. I stayed home from school to pick up pecans in November and December, so I almost failed the seventh grade. They said I did not have enough class-room time to pass, even though my grades were okay. I had picked up from fifty to a hundred pounds per day, at five cents per pound. Also, that year we had all the cousins come down for Thanksgiving and help pick up pecans. We did not have a turkey that year, but the day before Thanksgiving we all went squirrel hunting! You see, with all the pecans to feed on, there were squirrels everywhere. We killed twenty-seven that day cooked all of them for Thanksgiving. We all ate 'til we were full. That was the best Thanksgiving we ever had!

With all the cousins down, we played war with corn cobs and gourds in the hay barns. We made forts with the hay bales. We were having lots of fun until I hit one of the cousins right in the eye with one of the gourds. That gourd smashed and the juice went right into his eye. It must have burned like the dickens, because he ran crying to his mother. That was the end of our war games. Dad was a little upset that all the corn cobs were all over the hay.

There was one time during all that rain that Dad told me to go and get the shovel. He knew that I had been using it way on the other side of the barn and had left it there. So, he told me to go get it, and I told him, no, I was not going to go and get it. I thought it was too far away, and I should not have to go and get it. What got into me? I really don't know, but Dad said, "You *will* go get it right now, or you are going to get this belt!" Dumb me, I had to say "no" once again. And that was it. Dad took that belt off so fast I was not able to run away. He whipped me so much, that I started praying for him to stop. I must have gotten at least twenty licks from that. My legs were burned all the way up my back. When he turned me loose, I ran and got that shovel and never said no to him again. I think I was about twelve when that happened.

I was always trying new ways to earn money on the farm. During the summer, I would plow the fields for a quarter a day. I thought that was a lot of money at the time. During the fall, I would pick up pecans for five cents a pound. I would pick cotton for two cents a pound. I would use that money to buy my school clothes and shoes. I don't remember Mom and Dad buying any of my clothes after I was nine years old. We did not have all the games and toys and junk that kids have today. We learned how to be responsible and how to work.

At twelve years old, I wanted a .22 caliber gun. I saw one in the store and told Dad I would like to have that gun for Christmas. He said, "No, you can buy it yourself with your money." That gun was twelve dollars. So I gave him two dollars and asked if he could save it for me. We would go to town about every two weeks with a dollar or two and put money on that gun. It was a single-shot bolt action .22. I paid it off just before Christmas that year. Everybody was so proud of me, and I was proud of that gun. I still have it to this day.

At age thirteen, I was out for cotton picking. We were down in the bottom, next to the river, and the cotton was very good. On one occasion, I was picking two rows at a time, and this guy next to me was doing four rows and challenging me to keep up with him. Well, would you believe, this man picked over eight hundred pounds that day! I did 385 and made almost eight dollars. That was in 1958, and, at that time, that was a lot of money for me.

That same year, we went into the chicken business with about five hundred laying hens. In order to sell the eggs, we started an egg route in Oklahoma City. Every Friday, we would load up the car with several cases of eggs. We sold those eggs for fifty cents per dozen. That paid for the feed, and we still had money left over, so in the summer of '58 we decided to start saving all the extra coins in a big jar. With that money, we would take a trip to California to see our aunt in Stockton. In August of '58 we counted the money in that jar. We had over two hundred dollars in pennies, nickels, dimes, quarters, and a few half dollars.

Dad had bought a new Chevrolet. This car had no air conditioning; it was the cheapest model they made. We left on a Monday morning. Driving on old Route 66, we drove to somewhere in New Mexico. Dad got tired of driving, so he pulled over to the side of the road and slept for a few hours. In order to save money, we had brought a little cook stove to cook bacon and lots of eggs. Mom set that stove up and we had a good breakfast that morning. Cars and trucks went by and honked. I guess they wished they could have some of that good food.

On that Tuesday, we drove to the Painted Desert and the Petrified Forest. We had never seen anything like that before. You see, this was the first vacation we had ever taken! That was the only one while I was home. It was also the first time I had been out of the state of Oklahoma, except when Dad was in the service, and I was a baby.

Later, we were in the hottest part of Arizona. To keep the inside of the car a little cooler, Dad bought a great big block of ice and put it right in front of Mom's vent. It seemed to help somewhat. We stopped in Needles, California at about eleven at night, and it was still over a hundred degrees! Dad drove all night, and Wednesday morning at about eight, we arrived at our aunt's house. That was about two thousand miles from Oklahoma.

On that trip, we got to see the big trees and all the beautiful mountains. Dad decided he did not want to go back through Arizona, so we came back through Reno, Nevada and Utah and saw the Great Salt Lake. Then we came down through Denver and were back home in two days.

We had left the farm with our cousins. They moved into the house for the two weeks we were gone. They cleaned out the freezer and spent all the money they made on the egg route. We came back broke, so that week we ate lots and lots of eggs.

Finally, Dad and Mom decided it was time to move on. Dad found fifty acres up around Purcell, Oklahoma for three thousand dollars. It did not have a house on it, so he found someone who was selling his house. He moved it onto the property and built a chicken house. We moved in April of '59 to this house that had running water and a restroom inside. Dad and the landlord had decided it was time to part company. Dad wanted to do something else, and the landlord had lost over a hundred acres to the river. He thought it was time to sell the place and cut his losses. So, about June of '59, they had a big farm sale and sold everything from cows to all the equipment, plus the farm, in one day. By then we had already moved to our new house, just outside of Purcell.

At the age of fourteen, when I was in the ninth grade, I joined the FFA (Future Farmers of America). That first year, I had a pig as a project. We had a lot of pigs from that point on. We had several cows that we would put extra calves on so they would raise them as their own, but there was always one cow that we had to milk. It was my job to milk that cow for our milk to drink. I would get one gallon every day, and then let the calves get the rest.

My other job was to gather eggs from the chicken house. We would collect the eggs and then box them for sale for our egg route on Fridays. Mom would run this route during school. We enlarged the chicken farm in the fall of '60 by building a 30- by 250-foot chicken house that would hold somewhere around five thousand chickens. This chicken house had hens that were crossed with some big, old roosters. These kinds of eggs were used to hatch chickens for eating. They were very fast-growing and would be ready for market in four to six weeks. We got a bonus on the hatch rate. The higher the hatch rate, the more money we made. The worst thing was when those roosters would get so big, they would get downright mean! They would fight you when you would go to gather eggs. Those hens were not any better; if they were on the nest, they would peck your hand.

Dad was not afraid of work. He got a job in the city and would work 'til 4:30, and then he would go down to a welding shop and weld for five more hours, until ten. In '61 my Uncle Marvin bought a welding truck and asked Dad to start welding in the oil field. At that time, they would charge six dollars per hour, and dad would get two dollars per hour. Some days he would work around the clock to get a job done out in the field. When he came home, he was always busy doing something around the farm. Dad only went up to the seventh grade and, like me, could not read. So in about '46, one of the pastors from the church we were attending took an interest in Dad, and they began to read the Bible. Dad used to tell us that God taught him how to read. He said he could not pick up a book and read it. He read only the Bible for many years, but finally got to where he could read a book or the newspaper.

Every summer I was doing some kind of work to earn money. During the fall, usually in October, it was cotton-picking time. I would get out of school and ride my bike for the four miles to home and get my cotton sack and go and pick cotton 'til dark. I could pick about a hundred pounds in about three hours. Our neighbor, Mr. West, told me to come on and work anytime I was free. He liked how hard I would work. I would go home on my bike and be tuckered out, but I still had all the chores to do: let the calves in to feed and then put them back out, feed and water the pigs, pick up all the eggs. I did not study very much at home. I had one study hall and would get all my schoolwork done there.

On Sundays Dad would have to work, and so he would let me drive the car or pickup the seven miles to church when I was fourteen. It was a country church, so I did not have to worry about the police. I met a Jimmy Chriswell in the ninth grade. We had the same classes almost every year and became good friends. His Dad worked at the John Deere place in town, and he would ride in and then get his bike out and ride out to the house. That was during the summers of '59 and '60. We would go fishing in our pond and had a lot of fun together. At age fourteen, I was driving the old truck everywhere. That was an old 1949 Ford Flathead Six. It was one of those four-speeds that shifted from the floor. It would run like crazy. Anyway, I think Jimmy liked my younger sister a little, because in our senior year, he invited her for the sweetheart banquet. I drove over and picked him up, and then I went and picked up my date. I think that was my first date; neither one of us were into the boyfriend and girlfriend thing, even as seniors.

During the summer of '60, I got a job chopping cotton. You talk about a hot job! I made seventy-five cents per hour. That was the hottest job I ever did up 'til that time. In the summer of '61, I went to work for my uncle, hauling watermelons. He would pay me seven dollars a day. I worked seven days a week, and that lasted for eight weeks that summer. We would load a big, two-ton flatbed truck with about two hundred melons. Afterward, we milked about a hundred head of cattle. We would then take the load of melons to Oklahoma City, where we would deliver them to several different stores. We would get back in time to milk the cows again. I slept and ate there, going home maybe once during that time.

The summer of '62, I got a job washing windows for six weeks at the University of Oklahoma. The boss did not want to hire me because he said I was too little, but I told him I would do twice as much as any of the other guys, so he said, "Ok, I like you." I never disappointed him. One day we were washing windows at one of the class buildings, and all the guys started whistling. I turned to see what it was all about. Right in front of me was one of the prettiest girls I had ever seen. I was on a ladder, and I fell right off that ladder! I was so embarrassed. That job only lasted about six weeks. What was so much fun was that we would come in to the shop at 11:45, eat our lunch real fast, and, as soon as it hit noon, we would run over to the union building just across the street. We could play pool for a dollar. There were four of us guys; we all did everything together during those six weeks. I had never seen a pool table up 'til then. After six weeks, I got pretty good. We never bet on the games. We were there just to have fun. After those six weeks, I went back to work for my Uncle Carl for the rest of the summer.

When I was in the tenth grade, we got a new FFA (Future Farmers of America) leader by the name of Harry Franks. This guy would take us out on field trips almost every day to look at and judge cows and pigs. Then we would look at land and judge it as well. The way he impacted us the most was that he showed concern for each one of us, encouraged us to do better, and gave us determination that we were as good as anyone else in school. Most of us thought we would be just another farmer, but he encouraged many of us to go on to college. Many of my class- mates credit him as being the person who helped them climb higher. I know he was the one who encouraged me to do better. So, as a senior, I would do our class, and then I would take my study hall hours and come and help him with the ninth grade class.

During my junior year of high school, I really became interested in judging animals, land pas- tures, and plants. We had Mr. Franks as our teacher. He was really good at teaching us how to judge dif- ferent things. He would take us out to all these farms and show us what to look for in cows and pigs. Then we would go out and dig a hole and see how deep the topsoil was. Then he would show us what plants were good for cows to eat, as well as the characteris- tics of those plants.

We went to state in May of '62. I went as an alter- nate, and our team won the International Pasture and Range judging contest. I made up my mind that I was going to be on that team the next year, so I went out with the FFA teacher two different hours. I was only carrying four classes my senior year, so I had time to learn. We went to State again the May of '63 and won the International Pasture and Range contest again. Anyway, I won the first place overall. I got to be on TV for the first time!

Now you have to understand … I was a little, short kid in the twelfth grade, and nobody thought I was in the twelfth grade. When that FFA teacher called my name in the assembly in front of the whole school, everybody was asking who this little kid was! In 2013, I went back to Purcell for our fiftieth school reunion, and some still could not believe that I was in the same class as they were.

One thing we had done before we left high school was write what we thought we were going to do with our lives. It was interesting to hear what I had put down. I had written that I was going to be a chicken farmer in Arizona. I look back now, and I can say for sure that God has a destiny for each of us. I do live in Arizona, but I don't have any chickens, at least for now. I still like to see things grow. I look back at Romans 8:28 where it says, "And we know that in all things, God works for the good of those who love him, who have been called according to his purpose." (NIV)

I got out of school on May 20, 1963, and the following week went to work on a great big dam that was being built just east of Norman, Oklahoma. I was making a dollar twenty-five per hour. I became a helper and did whatever was needed. The biggest job was to help drill ten-foot holes in the rock and then set dynamite in them. That was in solid rock, where the spillway was to be built. We would drill from eight in the morning 'til about three in the afternoon. We would set the cap in the dynamite, and then we would drop three five-pound sticks in the hole with the cap wire out of the hole. We would tighten all these together and hook it to a long wire connected to the detonator. We would blow a warning and then blow it up at four that afternoon. During the night, the heavy equipment would come in and dig that out. We would do this over and over 'til we got down to somewhere around a hundred feet. After a few weeks of that, the boss gave me a raise to a dollar fifty per hour. I made enough to buy my first car, a 1956 Chevrolet, for four hundred dollars. I was so proud of that car. I also made enough to pay my way to college, Oklahoma Tech School in Okmulgee, for one year. There, I enrolled in Air Condition System Repair.

The first course I took covered basic electricity. I was trying my best to learn how all the amps, volts, et cetera worked. I was really having a hard time, but something happened one night at two in the morning. I guess I was dreaming, but I began to wire up these systems. All I know is that God showed me how it was supposed to work. I came in the next morning and started drawing it out on paper, and the instructor could not believe it! He asked, "Who helped you do this?" I said, "No one." He took that paper and gave me another one and said, "Do this one while I watch." From that point on, I started making A's in that class.

So after two semesters, I ran out of money and took the summer off to work in the air conditioning field. I took a job in Norman at Gordon's Air Condition and Heating. I hired on as a helper, and they put me to helping this guy who was putting add-ons onto the heating systems. My main job was to wrap vapor seals around the heating ducts in the attics. That was okay from April to about the first of July. Unfortunately, it became one of the hottest summers in Oklahoma, and for twenty-one days straight it was over 105 degrees, with humidity! By ten o'clock, those attics would be over 140 degrees and unsuitable for working.

Chapter 4

JOINING THE AIR FORCE

I n the middle of August, I made a decision to do something else. First I looked at the draft board to see where I was on the board. I was number thirty-seven. I told myself right then and there that I had better join quickly before they assigned me to the Army. So I joined the Air Force. It was August 31 when I went to Lackland Air Force Base. What an experience. Dad dropped me off in Oklahoma City at the induction center at six in the morning. There we did all the testing, and then came the physical. We all had to strip down to nothing, so the doctor could to do his thing. Need I say more? After a while, we were finally allowed to put our clothes back on. Then came the eye test. I was wearing glasses and could see pretty well, but the person told me I needed to go down a few blocks to see an eye doctor. I thought to myself … what now? Well, he signed off on my sheet and sent me back. So, they accepted me after that report.

From that time on, my nightmare began. They loaded us onto a bus and took us to the airport. There I got on my first airplane. Most of the guys got off the plane in Lawton to go into the Army at Fort Sill. We went from there to Dallas-Fort Worth and got on a jet plane to fly to San Antonio. We got off that plane and were met by a TI (Tech Instructor). This guy was the loudest and most vulgar person I had ever heard. Now, you have to understand, I went to church every week and did not talk like that at all. So it was a little hard to take; I was in shock from all this. This was at about one in the morning. The TI loaded us onto a bus which took us to a holding area for a few hours. He told us to get some sleep. But at four in the morning he came back and started with this loud yelling! He took us to some barracks where he said we were going to sleep for a few hours, but at five in the morning he woke us up, lined us up, and then took us to breakfast. Needless to say, I did not sleep at all that night. He brought us back to the barracks, telling us to shower and shave. I was not used to shaving, so while I was trying to put a blade in the razor, I cut my thumb and bled all over the floor. I took hell from the TI. From then on, I tried to stay on the quiet side and stayed out of his way. He never got on my case again.

After five weeks they sent me to tech school, where they told me I was going to a jet engine mechanic school in the Amarillo, Texas AFB. We got there the beginning of October. That first week some had to go to work in the lunchroom, which was called KP. They would get up at three in the morning and would not get back 'til nine o'clock that evening. For some reason this sergeant took a liking to me. Maybe it was because his last name was Lester, too. So, for that first week, I was able to go over to his hanger in the tool department and hand out tools. That was a real easy job. That was a ten-week course. It would just teach you the basic fundamentals of what a jet engine looked like. We trained on a J-57 engine, and then we would put one in an F-100 aircraft. Then we got a week on the test cell running engines. The thing I really remember was how cold it was there. In November, a snowstorm came, and that wind blew at least forty miles per hour, and the temperature dropped into the single figures. They said the chill factor was almost forty below zero. We put on every coat we could get our hands on and wrapped towels around our faces. That had to be the coldest winter I can ever remember.

We got off on a Thursday—December 24—to have leave to go home for Christmas. I took a bus from Amarillo, Texas to Oklahoma City. That bus stopped at every little town along the way and took about eight hours to get to Oklahoma City. I called home before I got on the bus, and Mom or Dad was going to be waiting for me at the bus station. I had to be back Sunday night by ten. I did not want to ride that bus back, so I asked Dad if I could use the car. It was a new 1965 Chevrolet. All my friends wanted to know who had driven that new car back to the base. They could not believe it when I told them I had. They wanted to know if we were rich or something. I told them that I didn't want to ride that bus again, and we only had two days to go! We graduated on December 28.

I was to report to Holloman AFB in New Mexico on January 11. After getting settled in the barracks, I drove to town about ten miles away and began to look for a church. The town was Alamogordo, New

Mexico. Mom had always told me to find a church as soon as possible. That year was real training for me to work on a new aircraft and engine. When I got there we had F-84 with the J-65 engines. Within a few weeks, we began to get our first F-4C from the factory. There was not a lot of work to do, so we would report for duty in the morning, and then they would dismiss us. That was nice for a few months.

Then the Vietnam War began to heat up, and we started having ORI (Combat Readiness). This is where we would plan to head overseas. We had to launch all the aircraft. We would bring all our equipment down to the ramp to load the C-141s and C-124s. We did this several times during the summer of '65. When October came, they told us to be ready, that this was the real thing and we would be leaving shortly. The first group left in October and the second one left in November. Our squadron was next on the list to go. They did not send us in December and told us to take leave for a few days, because when we got back, we could not go anywhere before we left. Well, we waited 'til January 21, 1966. They called us out at four in the morning. We still did not leave 'til two o'clock that afternoon. We loaded all our clothes, tool boxes, and foul weather gear. Plus, they gave us

M-16s to carry. There were about two hundred men with all our stuff on that plane.

The trailers and extra engines were loaded on the 124s. One of my friends was on one of those planes and it took him over a week to get to the Philippines at Clark AFB. I was on the C-141, and our first stop was in Hawaii at Hickman AFB. We Landed at about eight in the evening. We were very hungry, so they opened up one of the chow halls and fed us. That was one of the best meals we ever had. The next morning, we got another great meal.

Then we got on board to fly to Wake Island, a small island only about one mile wide by two miles long. The runway covers most of that island. We landed for fuel and lunch. The interesting thing that happened was that when we started down the runway, the pilot aborted and hit the brakes so hard I thought we were going to fly out of there.

He turned the aircraft around and came on the intercom and told us that one of the engines would not get over 80 percent. With our load, this was a critical issue. We headed down the runway again, and again he aborted. I know my heart was pounding, and I begin to really pray. We sat on the runway for several minutes, although it seemed like forever. Finally,

I thought all engines were running at full speed, and we started to roll again. I began to see the water and rocks, and, finally, that plane got off the ground with only a few feet left of the runway! We got in the air, and the pilot came back on the intercom and said we had only three engines at full speed, and the other one would not get over 80 percent.

Somewhere along the way, we crossed the international dateline. We arrived in the Philippines on a Tuesday morning. We had totally lost our Monday. We unloaded all our stuff, and they put us in a barracks. We were waiting for orders to go to Vietnam. After waiting for two weeks for someone to pick us up, the word came down that they had nowhere to put us up and that we were to start working in the engine shop at Clark AFB. Well, we had all these M-16s with us, and everybody was very concerned that someone would steal them. They said they were worth a tousand dollars on the black market. They finally decided to get all of them and lock them up. While stationed at Clark AFB, I found a church to go just outside the base. It was a Pentecostal Fellowship. They would have the men over for worship services and meals. That was the best part.

In February, we had to fly to Vietnam and sign in. So we got on a C-130 and flew to Cam Ranh Bay and signed in and flew out the next day, back to Clark AFB. First we had to fly to Thailand to pick some other personnel up. We had time to get off the plane, and right by the hanger was a Coke machine that had real Cokes for a quarter. I think we all got one. The Cokes in the Philippines just did not taste like Coke, even though these were bottled in the USA. Then we had to pick up TDY (temporary duty) orders back to Clark AFB. How crazy was that!

While in the Philippines, I was able to go to several places around the area. During Easter, on Good Friday, we went to a crucifix play of Jesus. There were all these men who cut their backs and then beat them with ropes with sticks on the end. They had sticks that were supposed to represent the cat o' nine tails that was used to beat Jesus. This would numb the back, but it would sling the blood everywhere. My shirt had spots of blood all over it. Then we watched them put the nails into their hands, and then they would tie them on the cross and let them hang there for about three hours. It was a sad thing to see.

My friend who I worked and bunked with and I decided we would go down to Manila to buy a refrigerator. Our plan was to ride the local bus for about two hours to downtown Manila. The trip cost about one US dollar. We would buy the unit and take it to Vietnam when we got to go back over. We finally found the place after going through the marketplace, which had shoulder-to-shoulder crowds. At any moment, I was expecting to be robbed. We found the appliance store. We paid 140 US dollars for the refrigerator and 20 US dollars for a transformer that went from 220 volts down to 120. Picture this ... here were two American guys in a crowd carrying this big box back to the bus station. By then it was about two in the afternoon, and many people and their chickens, goats, et cetera were all trying to get on the same bus. I had never seen such pushing and shoving in my life. That bus could only hold about forty-eight passengers. Finally, we gave this one kid two pesos, and he pushed his way in and got us a seat on that bus. There we were, sitting in our seat, with the refrigerator sitting on our laps, with chickens on all the overhead racks! The driver kept letting people on until there was standing room only. People were hanging out the door and on the back of the bus, and even on top. We had a few inches on our seat, and two people sat on that. I could not believe what we were seeing. We made it back to Clark AFB that evening. We carried that unit to Vietnam and set it up in our tent and had cold soda all the time. We sold sodas for twenty-five cents. Everybody wanted one of our sodas, especially in that heat! We sold the unit for what we paid for it, even after we used it all that year.

In Vietnam, I saw several planes that came back all shot up. The compressor would be just terrible, and we would ask the pilot if he had any problems with the engines, and he would say no. We would have to pull the engine and take the top of the compressor chamber off. Then we could see how bad the compressor was damaged. At times we could file the bad spots out, if it was not too bad. One day we got an engine in and the compressor was certainly damaged beyond repair. The main boss came and told us that they really needed those engines back in service and wanted to know if it was possible to have it on the ground in our eight-hour shift. At times we would do twelve-hour shifts and work from two to three weeks that way without a day off. Some would work from noon to midnight, and others would work from midnight to noon. I was blessed to go in at noon and get off at midnight. We were able to sleep in the morning, before it got too hot, so we told him we could do it. Up 'til then, it would take a four man crew about two days to do this. Well, my friend and I started at the back, and the other two men started loosening everything to separate the compressor halves. We got to working very hard and had that compressor in the container by the time our shift was over. That was without any power tools. I am sure you could do it now with power tools. Back then, no one with just a four-man crew had done this. I thought we might get something special award for doing that job so quickly, but we did not get a thing. Just a "good job" from the boss.

In October of '66, we got to see President Johnson. He came and drove right down the main street from the runway on his way down to the bay where the ships were docked. I think I was about twenty feet from where his car came down. Then during Christmastime, we had Bob Hope land at the base. He had Phyllis Diller and some other lady who was very pretty. At the same time Bob Hope was putting on his show, Billy Graham was preaching at our outdoor theatre. He had George Beverly Shea. He sang several songs. When he started singing "How Great Thou Art," I don't believe there was a dry eye in the group. He had a great anointing.

In our tent, we had sixteen men. Most of us worked in the evening, at about four in the afternoon. By nine in the morning, it was so hot you could not sleep. So we would go to the beach or just sit around and play cards. One of the guys found out I was from Oklahoma, and he told me he was too. Come to find out, he was the older brother of one of the guys I went to school with. One day he was a little drunk, and he told me to sit down and have a drink with him for old time's sake. I told him I did not drink, and he got real mad and was going to make me have a drink with him. Well, several of the guys told him to leave me alone. I thought we were going to have a fight right there, but they gave me a chance to get out of the tent. Several days later, the guy apologized to me. He said, "You are a better man than me. I wish I could resist temptation like you can." I got to witness to him. He did not accept Christ right then, and he went back to the states two weeks later. I do not know if he ever accepted Christ as his Savior. God's hand of protection was all around me during the four years I was in the service. I never drank nor smoked. I was always going to church or a prayer meeting.

At last we got orders to fly out on the plane. On January 11, 1967, we flew up to Saigon, Vietnam. We stayed overnight, and we heard bombs going off all night. I was getting a little concerned, so I did a lot of praying. We left Vietnam at nine at night on January 12. After one stop in Okinawa, Japan, we flew into California at 8 that night. We got our day back from crossing the International Date Line.

While in Vietnam, several of us got those "Dear John" letters. I got one in March, and she said she was going out with my best friend. That did not affect me too much, because I expected it to happen.

One of the friends I worked with was married, and he got one of those letters in October of '66. We had worked together for two years, and he was the one who went with me to get the refrigerator. We had bunked together in the same tent, but that day I had gone somewhere to do something else when he got his letter. Well, several of the other guys who were in the tent that day said he went off the deep end. He started screaming and hitting the locker and was like a wild man. Someone called the MPs and they took him to the hospital. I went down to see him a few days later, but he was so drugged up. It was sad. We talked, and he said they thought he was crazy. They sent him back to the states. I never heard from him again; I have tried to find him, but have had no such luck.

Next, I was assigned to Davis-Monthan AFB in Tucson, Arizona. Before I went into the Air Force, I was dating a girl from the town of Lexington, Oklahoma. So, while in Vietnam, I started writing her. When I got back to the states, I asked her to marry me. She agreed, and we got married on June 9, 1967. In about April, they asked me to go to driver's school and get a license to drive on the flight line. After going through all the classes, we had to pass an eye test. That was for night vision and depth perception. I was not able to pass the test, so the instructor told me to go get checked out with the eye doctor. Well, that was the day he said, "I can get you out tomorrow." I told him I was getting married shortly and did not want to get out right then. He asked me to come back later, but I never went back. At least he wrote down what was wrong, because a little later I filed for disability. My records showed what was wrong with my eyes.

In June of '67 my wife, Betty, moved with me to Tucson. We were so much in love. It did not matter that we had no money. We took care of a house for a few months, and then we moved into a little, furnished house. It cost us seventy dollars a month. By the time we got out of the Air Force in August, we had our first son, Robbie.

While in Tucson, I saw several plane crashes. One day I was standing on the ladder watching a F101 taking off. It was a National Guard plane from one of the states back East. It had two J57 engines with Afterburners. While going down the runway, something happened, and one of the engines caught fire. It began to burn through the outside of the plane. I knew something was wrong with that plane, because when he lifted off, the tower must have told him he was on fire. He began to make a right turn and come back to the base. I was watching things fall off that plane, and the fire was really increasing. He was able to line up with the runway on the south end, but he got about twenty-five feet off the runway before he lost control and could not bring it down. I was watching this plane not more than two hundred yards away from me. He did something I could not believe; he pulled the drag chute to slow the plane down, but what it did was flip upside down. He went right into the ground to the left. If that plane had flipped to the right, it would have hit some of our parked planes that were on the ramp. That pilot did not have a chance to get out of that plane. It was one of the worst crashes I had seen. I saw several planes in Vietnam come back and make a bellow landing, when the landing gear would not come down. We had this great big crane that would go out and lift the plane up when they could not get the gear down. They would bring it back out to the hanger and work on it. We called that crane the Praying Mantis.

We were in Tucson on the December 23, 1967 at about five thirty in the evening. I heard this F4 take off (we lived about six blocks from the end of the runway). I told Betty that something was wrong with that plane, because all of a sudden I heard nothing. I knew that when they would come out of afterburner the engine would still be so loud they could not hear each other talk. It about twenty minutes before we got through with supper and went down to Sears to do some more Christmas shopping. I went out the front door, and people are running up and down the street, telling everyone a plane had crashed into the Safeway store two blocks from the house. It killed five people in that store that evening. The pilots parachuted out and both were okay. Now the story goes that there was a new pilot in the back seat, and the pilot let him pull back the throttles. This was the first time he allowed him to do this. It is said that he was so excited to do so, that he pulled the throttles all the way back to shut off. That killed the engines, and they did not have enough altitude to restart the engines. That plane went down like a rock! It could have been off a few feet would have taken out a lot of houses. I always stand on the verse in Psalms 91 where it says His wings of protection will be all around us.

I had a crew of four men in '67 and '68, and we worked together really well. On one occasion the boss asked us to go pull both engines out of an airplane. It was normal for a crew to take four hours to take both engines out, but that day we were on a roll. We had both engines on the ground, ready to go back to the shop, in forty-five minutes. Our boss came back to help in about two hours, and we were sitting on our toolboxes waiting for him to bring the truck back. He could not believe his eyes. We had worked together enough that each of us knew what the other one was going to do.

One day we had a new man working with us. We were putting the engines back in the planes, and I was on the wing, trying to hook up the mount on that side. I kept telling him to turn it to the right to raise that side up. He kept turning and nothing was happening.

I told him to hold on and came down to see what he was doing. He was turning it to the left, and the dolly and pins had come loose from the engines and it was down about four inches from where it was supposed to be. I should have told him to turn the adjustment clockwise, and maybe that would have been a little easier for him to understand. I was a little upset, because I thought that engine would fall. I began to turn the adjustment to the right, and it came right back into the mount where it was supposed to be. I gave that young man a lesson in right and left and clockwise and counterclockwise. I still have nightmares about seeing that engine fall on someone!

At the end of our four years in the Air Force, they posted a bulletin about a two-week class for training to work at the post office. My friend, Bod Porter, and I went to that class for two weeks and finished it and took the test for the post office.

I put in for Oklahoma. I did not know what would come of it, but I made a score of 96, and with 5 extra points for time in service, it came to 101. I was at the top of the list.

Chapter 5

LIFE AFTER THE AIR FORCE

—⚬⚬⚬—

After I got out of the Air Force, I moved the family back to Oklahoma. We had borrowed my dad's Chevrolet Impala, which was much bigger than our Mustang. We had the trunk and backseat filled, and then we had a rack on top. We were a little overloaded. By the time we got from Tucson to El Reno, Oklahoma, the car was weaving all over the road. I thought we had a flat, so we pulled into a station to get it fixed. He took the tire off to inspect it and found that the rim had a crack about eight inches long. He said it was most likely from all the weight. I really did not know what could be so heavy, unless it was all of Betty's shoes. I think it was just one of those things that it was just a defect in the rim.

We moved into a little two-bedroom house in Lexington. I had put my applications in at the post office and Tinker Air Force Base, but we had not heard from them. So I took a job at a company called Unit Parts. This company would rebuild almost any part of a car that was under the hood. I worked there for six weeks and could not stand it. I was on an assembly line that rebuilt generators for the cars. My job was to press a bearing in the front housing and then put on a metal plate with three little screws. Finally, the post office called me in for an interview. I went to work there for $3.05 an hour, almost a dollar more. The boss at Unit Parts was a little upset with me. I worked my tail off at the Post Office that fall. Christmastime provided a lot of overtime, but after ten months, I knew I did not want to do that for the next thirty years. I had an opportunity to transfer to Tinker AFB. I went to work on an assembly line putting J-79 engine compressors back together. I did blading for a few weeks, and then I worked my way up to the balance machine.

After a few months, I got a promotion to WG 8. I was able to go to the test cell and run engines. That was much better than doing the same thing over and over on the assembly line. All that time, I kept trying to get down to the F-4 line. Nobody wanted to let me go even though I had all the experience. One day I took off to go to the credit union. The F-4 line was right there. So I just stepped into the office to ask if I could see the boss. His secretary said okay. I went in and told him what I did in the service and where I was then working and said I wanted to come and work on the F-4 line and nobody would listen. He said, "Where have you been? We need you right now!" He told me to be there that afternoon! Boy, did I catch hell when I got back! My boss was waiting for me. He said, "You got what you wanted. Get your toolbox and get out of here!" He was not a happy camper. I was certainly one of his best employees, if not the best. That was the day I got to go to the flight line and flight test. The first thing they told me was that they needed a man who could run the engines on the aircraft. My first day was in the cockpit of an F-4D on the trim pad. During the next three years, we worked many overtime hours with the Vietnam War going on, and the F-4 was the work horse. I spent most of my time on the trim pad, running engines.

During the post office time in '68, we bought our first house for ten thousand dollars in Moore, Oklahoma. We put a hundred dollars down, and our monthly payment was ninety-one dollars per month. We lived in that house for about eighteen months, and then sold it. We moved into a new trailer on my dad's property outside of Purcell, where I grew up. In '71 we had our second son, James. In '72, we bought my dad and mom's house that was next door and sold the trailer. One thing I did in '71 was I went back to college on the GI Bill. Now you have to understand, my days and nights would just run together. I was taking twelve credit hours, going two days a week, from four to ten at night. It would take our carpool an hour to get to work in the morning. We would get off work at 3:15, make a dash for school across town, then get home at about eleven at night. It was downright crazy. Plus, I would work on a bus route on Saturdays and Sundays for our church. I don't remember studying much. I do remember going to sleep in class many times.

All this caught up with me in September of '74. They called me in for my flight physical. That set in motion something I never expected. I went in and they checked my blood pressure, which was 160/110. I have never been overweight. I weighed 140 pounds and did not have any fat on me. I went in to see the doctor, and he said, "I see you have a little high blood pressure. I need to look in your eyes. We can see over fifty different diseases by just looking in your eyes." Well, he looked at my eyes over and over again, and I wondered what was going on. Then I started having flashbacks to that day in the Air Force when the doctor told me he could get me out tomorrow. My blood pressure was really going up then! Well, he left the room and came back with another doctor who looked at my eyes for several minutes. That's it. He said, "Where do you work?" I said, "I work at flight test." He said, "You don't anymore. You have something wrong with your eyes, and I am sending you to a specialist. I want you to go to your family doctor and get that blood pressure down. Take a week off." My doctor did not like how high my blood pressure was. He asked me what I had been doing. I began to tell him that I would get up at about four in the morning and ride to work in a carpool of about five guys and work ten hours a day and then on Tuesdays and Thursdays would get off work and head for school for six hours and get home at about eleven. I would go to church on Wednesday nights. Mondays I would work in the garden. Fridays I would mow the lawn. Saturdays I would go out visiting those on the bus route and then to church on

Sunday and Sunday night. He looked at me and said, "Son, you are burning the candle at both ends, and if you don't slow down, you are going to be in trouble with your heart."

I have found that Vietnam veterans who have PTSD do one of three things: they are either a workaholic, an alcoholic, or a drug addict. This subject is very interesting, and has been discussed over the years. I do not claim to be an expert on this, but I do know that I have a hard time just sitting and relaxing. Most of the time, I need to be up and doing something, or I sit there and go to sleep. I also have a need to get a job done before taking a break.

Back to the doctor. I took my note back to the boss, and he looked at it and said, "What am I going to do with you?" Well, when I did come back to work, he put me in the coffee shop for six months.

Chapter 6

THE BOMB SHELL

———

The next week I went to a specialist. He looked at my eyes and said, "You have Retinitis Pigmentosa (RP)." I asked, "What is that and what does it mean? He said, "Well, you are going blind, and most likely in about ten years you will not be able to see at all." This was the greatest shock of my life. Here I was, twenty-nine years old, with two small kids and a wife to support. I was really wondering what I was going to do.

At that time, they requested that I go and have a complete work up on my eyes at the Health Science Center in Oklahoma City. I made an appointment for eight in the morning, thinking that it would be over in just a little while. Well, this guy started working and taking pictures. He dilated my eyes and looked and looked at them. He told me he had a class that would be in at ten. There were about twelve students who all had to have a look, because most of them had never seen what RP looked like. That took two hours. He took me to lunch and then came back to do flashing lights to see if I had any night vision. He told me that I had none, and then he did a complete field test. Everything was less than fifteen degrees. With my glasses, I could see 20/40 in one eye and 20/60 in the other eye. I did not know you were considered legally blind at 20 degrees or less. There I was, driving everywhere—night and day. I did not think I had a problem, and I certainly did not want to give up that independence!

I had to be at school that afternoon at four. Since I had just gone through six full hours of testing, I could hardly see anything, but by the grace of God, I made it the twenty miles across town to the school. I was so tired in the first class that I laid my head down on the desk and slept most of that three-hour class. The guys I had been going to school with began to ask me what was wrong, and I told them about all those tests I had on my eyes that day. During last class, I was able to stay awake with some help from some coffee and was able to drive back home okay.

But all those reports went to the VA (Veterans Affairs). It took eighteen months to get everything approved. I began to spend several hours a week praying, asking God for an answer. I continued quoting Romans 8:28, where Paul tells us that all things work together for those who love him. I know the Word of God and my faith in God have sustained me through all this. I was really in the pit at that time.

One day while making coffee, one of the guys was telling me he had gotten disability from the VA. He said I should go see this service officer down-town. So, I made an appointment to go see him one afternoon. This guy had a lot of bad language. Every other word was a curse word. I told him the story about what the doctor said, plus what the doctor had said in the service. He typed it all up and told me to sign it. I looked at him and asked, "Do you think I have a chance of getting this claim through?" He said, "God only knows."

Back to the coffee shop. I was studying and taking fifteen credits that spring semester of '75. When the boss came down and began to talk to me, he told me about all the research he had been doing. He said, "We don't have any jobs for you." This was before the Disability Law of '93. He said, "The only thing we can do is retire you." This news was a real shock to me at that time. I just could not imagine what I was going to do. I asked for time to think about it. I went to my pastor and began to tell him what they wanted to do. He asked me some very important questions that I will never forget. "What do you think God wants you to do? You have been going to school for a reason. What are you going to do with the education? Can you use it where you work now?" That really got me to thinking about all my options. I could retire on the disability. Would I be willing to step out of my comfort zone and go for it, or should I try and stay and see if they could come up with something else?

I went over to personnel and started the paperwork to retire. The human resources person said, "They will not approve this. You are too young and you have too much education." I told her I was going to go into the ministry, and she just gave me a funny look and said, "We shall see." Well, would you believe that in six weeks that application was approved! When I was checking out, she had to sign off on the paperwork. She could hardly believe her eyes. She said, "I have never seen one of these approved this fast." I just smiled and said, "Thank you."

I took that chance and retired in May of '75. At that time I drew 40 percent of my salary, which was not much. The scripture kept coming to me where Paul says, "I can do all things with God's help." Also, the scripture that comes from Philippians: "I can do all things through Christ who strengthens me," and "God is my provider." It was a great comfort to me to hear that scripture over and over in my mind. We should all stand on this scripture, when God calls us to do something. We should say, "With your help, I will do my best." But instead what happens is the devil starts to working on our minds and saying, "You can't do that!" and we allow fear to come into our minds. Then we just sit still and miss the opportunity God has placed in front of us. We miss the joy of helping someone in need. Some people will say that God has to speak to them out loud or God has to have someone to tell them what they should do. Most of the time, though, it is just that God gives you a suggestion to do something.

Remember the story of Elijah, when he was in the cave waiting on God. There was a powerful wind and God was not in it. Then there was an earthquake and fire, but God was not in those either. But then all was quiet and God spoke in a still, small voice, and Elijah knew that was God speaking to him. If we get in our closets and pray, God will speak to us. The hardest part for all of us, though, is to wait on the Lord. Isaiah, the prophet, said, "They who wait upon the Lord shall renew their strength. They shall mount up with wings as eagles. They shall run and not be weary."

We have to take this scripture to heart and believe that all things work together for the good of those that are called according to his purpose (Romans 8:28). Sure, we mess things up. Like the old time pastor told me, "You cannot put scrambled eggs back together, so stop trying, and go on and learn from that lesson."

I was going to school on the GI Bill, and I had about eighteen months left on it. So I knew I had that money coming in, but I did not know about the VA yet.

To save money, I sold our new car and bought an old car that had a damaged right side door. The guy wanted two hundred dollars for it. It was a '66 Plymouth with 62,000 miles on it. I found a door at a junk yard for twenty-five dolllars. We put it on and it really looked funny, because it was a yellow door and the car was green. The door did not fit really well, but we drove the wheels off that car for the next five years, driving it to Florida and back, to St. Louis, and then to Colorado. I gave the car to a military guy, and he drove it for about a year. He called me one day, saying I could come and pick up the car, because it needed some repairs and he did not have the money to repair it. So I took a battery out to the car, started it, drove it to the shop, and put a new muffler system on it for about seventy-five dollars. I drove it a while longer, until someone wanted to buy it for two hundred. So I sold it to him. That was one good car!

From '75 to '78 I finished up my degree. I had been going to a school in Oklahoma City called Southwestern Bible School. I had gotten 103 hours of college in Bible and Business Management. Everybody I talked with told me that not one four-year college would take all those hours. I was asking God what I should do, and he brought to my memory the University of Science and Arts about thirty-five miles west of our house in Chickasha. I took my transcripts over and talked to the dean. He looked them over and told me that he would take all the hours and give me a degree in Business Management if I would do thirty more hours. So, in '76 I was able to graduate with a BS in Business Administration.

During that time, I was trying several things on the farm. I bought about a dozen calves one September and was going to winter them and sell them in the spring. Calves usually go up in price at that time. That is what I was counting on. Well, that winter was a bad one. I had to buy extra hay to feed those calves—a lot more than I had expected. When I got ready to sell them in the spring, I just broke even. So I did not try that again. In '75 I bought out an old bee keeper for about five thousand dollars. The banker thought it was a good buy. He had been a bee keeper in Arkansas and made some good money. He thought I could do so. At that time I had several hives of bees, and that brought me up to about seventy-five hives of bees. I started splitting the hives and putting a new queen with each new hive I had split off. By '78 I had about 150 hives of bees. I had three trailers with twenty-four hives on each one. During the summer, I would move them from one field to another. I made some real good honey and never had any trouble selling it at the stores in town. Most years I broke even. I thought God just wanted me to make money to support the church, because I was always coming up with ways to make money.

During the end of '75 the VA approved me for disability and gave me a grant to buy a car. We bought a '76 Mercury Cougar, and it was the nicest car we ever had. We drove the wheels off that car, going back and forth to school five days a week. One month my gas bill was $175, and gas was only thirty-five cents a gallon! I would be surprised if that car got ten miles to the gallon of gas.

In August of '76 we had gotten some back pay and decided to go on a long vacation. We planned for three weeks off, so we headed out and stopped at White Sands in New Mexico. We let the boys play for a while on the sand. From there we showed the boys where we lived in Tucson, Arizona. Then we went up to the Grand Canyon and looked down to the river. I was holding on to the boys so tightly. They just wanted to get a little closer to the edge. We got to the rail and my head began to swim, and I just had to back off. That is one deep canyon! I do not think I could ever take a trip down to the bottom. From there we headed for Los Angeles and Disneyland. We spent two days there. Then on the third day I was trying to get on the I-5 and head north. It was about nine in the morning, so I figured all the traffic would be gone. What a surprise—those lanes were so packed you could not get in. Traffic was backed up so much that it took about two hours to just get out of town. I told Betty I was never going to live in Los Angeles. When we had come down the mountain from Victorville, you could see all the smog over the city—another minus. We hit 99 going north to Bakersfield. We were going to see Betty's sister in Marymount, California. We spent one week with her, and she took us to the big trees. It seemed like we went all over those mountains, and we saw several parks. We saw the big tree that you could drive a car through. That was one big tree! After that week we went north, across the Golden Gate Bridge, and over to Route 1, which goes up the coast. We drove that beautiful route all the way to the Washington border, stopping several times to take pictures. At that point, there was this really high bridge we needed to cross. I saw about one quarter of a mile up the bridge and told Betty that we were not going to cross it. It was all fog, and it just sent chills up my back. We took the road back over to I-5 and went through Seattle, Washington, right by the Needle. We headed for Canada, just to say we had been there. We drove a little ways into Vancouver, Canada. We just turned around and drove back into the US and stayed in a small town. We hit the road going to Spokane, Washington, and then to Idaho and on over to Montana. Somewhere in Montana, we stopped at a rest area to have lunch. We had brought sandwiches with us. We got all set up, and, all of a sudden, the mosquitoes hit us so fast. These things were the biggest ones I had ever seen, and we have a lot of them in Oklahoma. They got all over James, our youngest. He was five at that time. We ran for the car, and I threw everything back in and left that place. We ate the rest of our lunch in the car. Next we drove over to Yellowstone Park and stayed two nights. We saw bears, deer, elk, and several water-falls. On the last day, we went by the geyser to see it go up. We got there and in about five minutes, there it came! We did not stay outside very long, because it started snowing. We headed down the mountain and ran out of the snow, which turned to rain. We then headed for Cheyenne, Wyoming, and Denver, Colorado. We found the "North Pole," and the boys just loved it. We also saw the Royal Gorge and Pikes Peak. By then we had been on the road about three weeks and were ready for home.

I kept that car for about one year, and sold it after 44,000 miles. I bought a '77 Ford Courier pickup. I needed something besides a car to haul the hives back to the house in order to extract the honey. That pickup got thirty-plus miles to the gallon. That gas bill really went down. One day Betty had to go to school and said she had a quarter of a tank of gas. She asked if that was enough to get there and back, and I said that it should be. On her way back, she was two miles from the house and ran out of gas. That was the last time she ran out. After that, I made sure there was enough gas.

One night Dad and I were moving two loads of bees from Pauls Valley to Lindsay, which was about twenty-five miles. He was ahead of me in his truck and I was in a little pickup. We were going down a very long hill, and the trailer began to push me faster and faster down that hill. I was up to fifty miles per hour, and all of a sudden the sky just seemed to explode right in front of me. I thought I had lost the load of bees. I did not know for sure what happened. Then suddenly it looked like a big bolt of lightning hit the highway right in front of me! Boy, did I begin to pray. There I was in a storm, with a runaway truck that I could not slow down. I thought for sure I was going to run right over Dad. He saw me moving up on him, so he sped up, and we finally got to the bottom of that long hill. I was sweating bullets, but all was safe when we got to the field.

During those three years, we had gotten several more buses and were running 100 to 130 kids on those buses. Each summer we would take the kids down to Sulfur. We would take thirty to forty kids each summer down there and camp out. We would take all their bikes in a horse trailer and load the bus down with kids. Sometimes we would have to take two buses for all the camping equipment. We would have Bible study, bike riding, hiking, and swimming in that cold water. One year we were down there and in came a terrible storm. The wind was blowing and there was lightning and thunder. The kids were very scared. I think a lot of them went onto the bus and waited out the storm.

One year Betty was driving the old Plymouth that had a camper on the back, and the gas pedal stuck and she did not know what to do. So she rode the brakes, trying to slow the car down. We came into Davis, Oklahoma, and she had to stop. She could not get it to stop and ran into an old pickup. She stopped then. I knew something was wrong, so I had pulled over. That pickup was not even damaged. It had one of those really heavy duty bumpers. The car bumper hit it just right and did not do any damage to the car at all, but she would not drive it again. So I had to drive it home. I got it home and sprayed some silicone on it. We never had another problem with that gas pedal.

We would always plan a youth trip every summer, and we would go to churches and sing. We went to Christ of the Ozarks. One morning we were having breakfast at one of the restaurants to start our day. With us were these two guys named Bob and Bob, and they were always joking around. That morning one of the Bobs was giving his order like he wanted everything. For some reason this lady got upset, and suddenly they came out and told us that she had just quit. To this day Bob does not know what he said to upset that lady. Sometimes Bob had a way of getting under people's skin, but he certainly did not mean anything by it. What I think he wanted was his eggs cooked just right and asked for several other things he wanted with his meal. He was taking his time giving the order, and she was very concerned that she would not be able to handle all thirty of us. I bet something else was going on also. On one trip we were coming back home, and it was hotter than blazes. We did not have any air conditioning on the bus. Brother Thompson was always our driver. It was about three in the afternoon and some of the boys wanted to pour some ice water on Brother Thompson. They kept after me to let them do it. So I finally let them. It was a wonder we did not have an accident. Boy, was he was in shock over that ice water bit. Even so, Reverend Wayne Thompson was kind enough to write the following later:

> In June 1968 I, with my wife, moved to Purcell, Oklahoma to accept the pastorate position of Memorial Assembly of God Church. We had no experience in pastoring and our resumé was rather short. We had served two years as youth leaders for a local church and seventeen months preaching at revivals. When we moved to Purcell, it was like the beginning of a new life. The best thing I had going for me was that I believed this move was in the perfect will of God. So I knew the Lord was on my side, and also my wife was very committed to the Lord's work. So how could I fail?

The church at Purcell had about sixty people when we agreed to be their pastors. We began to pray for new people, and the Lord heard our prayers. Almost immediately we had four new couples move into town and start attending the church.

Margaret and Reve Bates were new to our area. They came to teach in the public school system in Wayne, Oklahoma. Both Margaret and Reve taught Sunday school classes for several years, while Reve served on the deacon board.

Mary and Joe Kennedy with their children soon showed up at Memorial Assembly. They were transferred to Purcell by Joe's Employment. They were faithful to God's house and served for several years as Sunday school teachers. Mary also served as a leader in the Missionettes, which is a program for girls. Joe also served as Sunday school superintendent and as a leader in the Royal Rangers, a program for the boys.

Zella and Roy Tyler, with their children, soon began to attend Memorial Assembly. The Tylers were the only couple who were former acquaintances. They had previously attended Trinity Assembly of God in Oklahoma City. The pastor of Trinity happened to be my sister and brother-in-law, Imogene and Walter Richmond. I received Jesus Christ as my Lord and Savior at Trinity Assembly in August of 1961. Zella and Roy Tyler were faithful to the Lord's house and served as teachers for many years. I believe Roy also served as church secretary, but, most of all, they were willing and faithful altar workers.

Betty and Ron Lester were perhaps the first of the new couples to start coming to Memorial Assembly. This couple proved to be a great blessing to the church and to us as pastors. During their ten-year stay at Memorial, we developed a friendship with them that has lasted for a lifetime. The Lesters were very faithful to the church and eager to serve the Lord. Betty served as a Sunday school teacher, a leader in Missionettes, and as church secretary. She also served as chaperon for youth trips and was faithful to help when we took the children on five-day camping trips. She also sang in the church choir.

Ron served as a chaperone for youth trips, as the Sunday school superintendent, and was a member of the church choir. But to me, he is best remembered for his bus ministry. He came to me and said, "If I can get a vehicle, can I start a bus ministry?" I had no idea what would happen, but I said, "Okay by me." Someone in the church gave him an old van. He had it painted, got a driver, and started a bus route in Purcell. Before he moved, the church owned five buses. He ran routes in Purcell, Lexington, Noble and Washington, Oklahoma. While he was director of the bus ministry, we broke the attendance record several times. I believe the Sunday of our final record breaking, we had 308 in attendance. We gave God the glory, but without Ron, it would not have happened.

Ron was good for me, because he always seemed to have an undying zeal. It seemed that when I would express my disappointments or frustrations to him, there would always be a burst of enthusiasm springing from him. During his time as the director of the bus ministry, we attended several bus conventions, and we received some good advice from people who had successful bus ministries. But I give Ron most of the credit for the success of our bus ministry at Memorial Assembly.

There was a time when I called him "Norman Jr." He read several of Norman Vinson Peale's books on enthusiasm. But Ron's zeal came from a different source, as it came from a heart that was on fire for

God. It was kindled by an overwhelming love for the Lord.

My feelings for Ron are founded on our close fellowships for the most of ten years. Yet, when I talk to him now, I realize the fire is still burning.

Most people have the tendency to allow the fire to lose its fervency as they get older, but not Ron. Some thirty five years have passed, and the fire still burns. Through the years his eyesight has continued to fail, yet his passion for God's work is as great as ever. Most people would have given up, but not Ron. The fire still burns.

When it comes to serving the Lord, Ron always seemed to give his best effort. This was true, whether he was singing in the choir or praising God or praying. He always appeared to be giving it his all. With sincerity, I deeply respect him and

take my hat off to him. Surely his reward
will be great.

His Friend Forever,
Wayne Thompson

Chapter 7

GOING INTO
THE MINISTRY

———∞∞∞———

From 1975 to July 1978 was decision time. In 1976 I finished my degree with a major in Accounting and Management, plus a major in Biblical Studies. I was not sure what I really wanted to do. I bought the small bee business and thought that was what God would have me do. I really liked to work with the bees and to see how they worked together to make all that honey. I was making some money selling my honey, because a lot of people wanted it. This only took a little of my time, and it wasn't making that much that much money. So I needed to find some other source of income. We lived on fifty acres, with plenty of grass, so we tried raising calves. My dad and I bought twelve head of cattle that September and kept them over the winter. The sad thing was, it snowed so much that winter, we had to buy hay and sack feed for those calves. Then spring came and the price of cattle dropped, so we did not break even on that project. Then I bought some worms and was going to do worm farming. People would tell you all the good things they could do with worms. Well, none of that worked out. When we went to see how many worms were in the beds, we could only find a few. It is funny, when we look back and see all the times we failed at something. But the saying goes … if you never try, you certainly will never have any success at anything. We learn by our mistakes, and I have made many of them over the years.

My pastor was very kind to me asked me if I would do visitation for him. So I went to the hospitals and the shut-ins. I was doing visiting for the bus ministry on Saturday, which would last most of the day. He offered me fifty dollars per week, to help with the gas. I really enjoyed that. I kept praying and asking God to give me a real direction.

In July of '78, I was moving a load of bees early in the morning. You should always move bees at night, when they are all back at the hive. Well, that morning we got about a mile down the road and hit a hole.

One of the main brackets broke loose and dropped some of the hives down. We knew we had to turn around and go back to the house and get the trailer fixed. That meant that we had to unload the hives and fix the trailer. Something happened that morning. It was like a vision or something. It was God talking to me. It was like he was saying, "Are you going to do what I have called you to do, or are you going to keep running, looking for other things to do?" Never before had God put something like that on my heart. It is something that you just know that you know that you have got to move on.

I had been talking about being a bus director to my pastor during that time. We had bought five buses and had over 130 kids coming to church on those buses. This was in the small town of Purcell, Oklahoma. We were considered one of the fastest-growing churches in Oklahoma at that time. We were breaking records of all kinds, and God was really moving in our services. We saw several miracles take place because we were praying. We had looked at going to a bus director school in Louisville, Kentucky. Then one day I called the pastor we had in Tucson, Arizona. He suggested I call a pastor in Arnold, Missouri. He had recently started a school that was basic training for ministers. Early that morning, I felt God press me to go to Arnold, Missouri and check it out. After unloading the bee hives, I went and told my wife that we were going to Arnold, Missouri ... to get up and let's go! So, in one hour we were on the road to Missouri. We got there, and they were not able to meet with us until after a prayer meeting at nine in the evening. In the meantime, we were looking for a hotel to stay in. Every place we called just so happened to be full that weekend. I was telling Pastor Brown about the situation, and he told me it was not a problem—they had several families that could take people in. They put us with a retired couple with the last name of Lucas. Come to find out, their son was a famous movie person and owned a horse ranch in Lexington, Oklahoma. I knew of the ranch, because we had picked up kids on our bus route in that same area. We had our meeting at the church after prayer. They had prayer from nine to ten every Saturday night. I liked what I saw. We told him we would pray about it.

We went back to Purcell, Oklahoma and began to make plans to move to Arnold, Missouri for one year to train to become a full-time bus director. We moved a lot of our furniture into a storage building and packed what we could into a twelve-foot trailer and two cars. We had to make arrangements for one of the guys in the church to take care of the bees for the rest of the summer and fall. He would need to take the crop of honey off about the first of October, so I left our truck with him to do this.

As we were driving down the road on Highway 44, I began to pray and ask God if I was doing the right thing. As I was praying, the song "I Will Follow Thee" came to me. As I sang that over and over, the presence of the Lord came down in that car, and I began to cry like I never had before. I could hardly see the road, but I began to feel such peace over our decision. I could hardly wait to get there and get started with training.

This was at the People's Church in Arnold, Missouri, with Pastor Kenneth Brown. This man was like a T.I., so I felt like I was back in the military. He was very organized. We were required to be involved in every part of the ministry, from buses, to children's ministry, to choir, to visitation. We were there Tuesday through Sunday. The only times off were Mondays and Fridays. School would go from seven in the morning to 12:30, and then we were off 'til six. Most of the guys had to work during that time to make ends meet. I did some work at the church, filling in here and there and running errands for the pastor.

My first assignment was to help someone on their bus route. I did not think I could get much benefit out of that, so I asked if I could have my own route. During my interview with the bus director, I told him I also wanted to be a bus director and needed to be somewhere I could really have an impact. I wanted to get a really good recommendation from him. So I asked him what I needed to do to get recommend to another pastor as a bus director. He said, "If you can build a bus route to fifty, I believe you can become a great bus director."

Chapter 8

ROUTE 13

———∞∞∞———

Well, I took on Route 13 that had only twenty-one kids on the best day. We took the map out, and he showed me where the route was. I went out and drove that route and prayed over it. We would go out on Saturday and start knocking on doors, and kids just came out of the woodwork. We came to one apartment complex and got about twenty kids to come. That first Sunday we came in late by about thirty minutes, but we had over seventy kids on that one bus. The driver was so excited. The director was so happy that he gave us another bus the next Sunday. We were able to build that bus route to over 130 that year. That earned us an award called the 100 Club, which few had the honor to be a part of.

On the first Sunday of May, I was to take all of our kids skating down by Fenton, Missouri. The kids all invited all their friends, and we had over 130 that day. We only had two buses on that route for that day. So we asked if we could have another bus, because there was standing room only. The bus director did not have another driver, so I told him I would drive. You see, I was still driving a car, and I would drive the buses around the lot. I thought I could do this, even with my vision problem. The director knew I had a vision problem, but I had talked him into letting me take the bus with thirty-eight kids on board. I drove in the middle of the other buses, and we made it to the skating rink and had a great time. We loaded back onto the buses at about 2:30 in the afternoon. and started back to Arnold, Missouri. After about five miles on a really curvy road, we came to a very sharp curve, and I misjudged the road. The back wheels fell off the road, and that caused the bus to roll over. As the bus rolled over, everything went into slow motion and my life just flashed before me. All I could think about was how many of these kids would be killed or hurt. I could see the newspapers: "Church Bus Kills Several Kids." I fell out of the driver's seat and went about halfway to the back of the bus. We were totally upside down, and I began to smell gas. The gas tank was up in the air and was leaking right into the cab of the bus. I knew we had to get out as fast as we could. I tried the front door and could see that was no use. That door was right up against a telephone pole and would not budge. I looked at the back door, which was right up against a big pile of dirt. It was a hot day, and all the windows were down on the bus. I began to tell the kids to crawl out through those windows. I checked to make sure all the kids were out. The bus behind us came to a stop and was just running up to help, and someone called for an ambulance and the police. The police wanted everyone to be checked out at the hospital. They transported every one of the kids to the hospital and did exams and x-rays, if the doctor thought there might be a broken bone. We had no broken bones, no cuts big enough for stitches, and there were few bruises. There was one girl that had hit the seat in front of her, and she had a pretty good bruise. That father was pretty upset. The insurance company gave him a thousand-dollar check, and he was satisfied. All the doctors and nurses were in total amazement as they examined the kids. They just could not understand how that bus could roll over and not really hurt anyone. I was a little bruised up physically, but I was really depressed over the mishap and very concerned about what the pastor would say and how the parents would react. The interesting thing was that the newspaper called me and was really trying to figure out what had happened. I just kept telling them that it was a miracle. You would think that article would have been on the front page, but it was on the second page, and a very short one at that.

The next Sunday was also a miracle, because we had thirty-two parents from Route 13 that came to church, plus one of the nurses from the hospital. Our bus director, David Earls, has told that story at many conferences. Why did the parents come? One of the reasons was that the three boys that made it out first began to tell the story that they had seen angels holding hands around the bus as they were climbing out. So that story spread like wildfire. I have no doubt that really happened, because that bus rolled over and landed on its top and it seemed like we had landed on a pillow. It was a very soft landing. We were doing about thirty-five miles per hour. We looked at the highway later, and that was the only place that bus could have turned over without rolling down a steep incline. I do believe that God was protecting us. Needless to say, I never drove another bus with kids on it.

Several of those children are now in the ministry, so I know that had a great impact on those children and their parents.

Here is an account of the bus accident that was written by Reverend David Earls, Pastor of Faith Assembly of God in Sullivan, Missouri:

ROUTE 13

The phone rang. I, David Earls, was sitting in my office on May 6, 1979, waiting for the buses of Route 13 to return from a special activity following Sunday school. The tone of the voice was one that every bus director fears. Tom, co-captain of the route said, "Brother Earls, the bus behind me has just turned over ... "

The bus had 39 people on board, including the driver and bus workers. My thoughts were, as I drove to the scene of the accident, "The ministry is destroyed. I might as well give up. There won't be anyone riding the buses anymore. There's no use trying. What am I going to do?" I did not know any details of the accident ... how many children had been hurt or anything.

When all examinations had been completed at the hospital, the doctor's report was, "Not a stitch, not a broken bone. We don't understand it. We don't understand." The news media carried the bus driver's testimony, "A Miracle of God."

On Monday morning following the accident, Rick, a twelve-year-old boy who had been on the bus, came to my office with his father to relate to me what he and his friend had experienced. They were the first ones to climb from the bus. "When we emerged from the wreckage," Rick stated, "we saw angels surrounding the bus, holding hands." Then I could understand the doctor's report.

According to Sheryl Deakins, one of the workers on the bus, the children were singing at the time of the accident. As their young voices filled the air with "I've Been Redeemed, By the Blood of the Lamb," He sent His angels to keep charge over them. (Incidentally, Sheryl is now married to my son, Arvel Earls. They have two children, Joshua and Olivia . Sheryl is teaching at People's Christian Academy, and both she and Arvel are actively involved in the ministry of People's Church).

The Bus rested on its top in a totaled condition. One tiny spark could have ignited the fuel that had poured into the bus, and all could have perished in a split second. But God. Oh but God had His hand upon them and dispatched His angels to keep charge over them and protect them, for He knew where he wanted these little ones to minister unto Him. Psalm 91:11 says, "For He shall give His angels charge over thee to keep thee in all thy ways."

Galatians 6:9 states: "And let us not be weary in well doing for in due season we shall reap if we faint not."

Within two weeks after the accident, a large amount of money was given to the bus ministry for the on-going of winning souls for Jesus. The buses would run to bring boys and girls and moms and dads to church.

Shortly after the accident, a little girl began riding the church bus to Sunday school. Her grandfather, Joe Devesconi, was the supervisor at MK bus lines. (Since the accident, we had started renting buses each week from MK Lines because of operational expenses). Joe was a retired serviceman. We could do nothing to please him. He was continuously using God's name in vain. Then one day, Joe had a heart attack and nearly died. While visiting him in the hospital, we were able to lead him in a sinner's prayer, and he accepted the Lord Jesus Christ as his personal savior and Lord. God began a healing in his body and soul. After his recovery, he began to attend church regularly and was baptized in water.

A short time later, Joe came to the church office and said, "Brother Earls, I need to talk with you." He said, "I am to receive a raise at my job, and I want to give my raise toward two rental buses to pick up boys and girls." With tears in his eyes he said, "And I want to be the driver of one of them on a route." He told me it was the dedication and faithfulness of the workers who came Sunday after Sunday to pick up the buses that influenced him. He saw Christ in them. He wanted what they had. Joe's attitude had changed. 2 Corinthians 5: 17 — "Therefore if any man be in Christ, he is a new creature. Old things are passed away; behold all things are become new." Today Joe Devesconi is faithfully attending church in South St. Louis, Missouri.

Eight years later while pastoring in Geary, Oklahoma, I invited a youth choir from Del City, Oklahoma, to come and minister in our church. The honorarium was to go to a young lady in the choir who was going on a MAPS trip to Mexico. When visiting with the young people, the young lady going on the MAPS trip thought she recognized me. When old acquaintances were renewed, I found she indeed was one of the children on the bus the day of the accident. Now, eight years later, she was to go on a mission field and minister to people who need Jesus. Because of Michelle's love for Jesus and her faithfulness to Him, her family has been saved and is living for the Lord today.

At this writing, Ron Lester, the bus captain of Route 13, is now pastoring West Shores Assembly of God church in Salton City, California. His son, James, is attending Evangel College in Springfield, Missouri, preparing for ministry.

Let me return to Rick, the twelve year old boy who came to my office that Monday morning. He has been enrolled in Oral Roberts University and is involved in the ministry of Home Bible Studies.

We are now approaching the twelfth anniversary of that tragic day for Route 13. When I began to recount all the good things that have come from Bus Route 13, they far outweigh the bad. It was truly "A Miracle of God." The devil meant to do harm, but God, in His goodness and mercy, turned it around for good. Several years have passed, and I cannot say that every one of the 131 boys and girls are living for the Lord; however, I can say many of them are, and several of them are in the ministry, continuing the winning of souls. Psalms 126: 5 & 6 — "They that sow in tears shall reap in joy. He that goeth forth and weepeth, bearing precious seed, shall doubtless come again with rejoicing, bringing his sheaves with him."

Should Jesus tarry, I know several others
will come to know Jesus as their Lord and
Savior. He doeth all things well.

The rest of my year in Arnold was spent running the five hundred miles back and forth to Purcell,
Oklahoma to take care of the bees. We had over 150
hives, and someone had to work them. So I would
take off after Sunday service, head for Purcell, and get
to Dad and Mom's house around ten at night. I would
get up early and go work on the hives, checking them
to see if there was need for more room. If bees get
too crowded, they make queen cells. When the new
queen comes out, the old will take off with about
one-third of the worker bees and start a new hive.
The place they start queen cells is right on the bottom
of the frame, in the bottom box. You have to unstick
all the boxes and look at the bottom box for those
queen cells. The reason you use a smoker is to make
the bees think the hive is on fire. They all go fill up
with honey, which makes them very slow and easier
to work with. I had some hives that would get very
upset and would sting you anyway. I had one hive
that got so mad at me I had to get under the truck and
wait them out. I got over a hundred stings that day;

several got inside my screen and stung my face. My eyes were all swollen up, and my ear was really large.

One week my wife, Betty, was helping me extract honey in our honey house. She hated those bees. I had gotten to where I could not drive at night very well, so she was driving back home when one of those bees got in the cab of the truck and started climbing up her leg and stung her good. Well, she stopped that truck right in the middle of the road screaming. She finally killed that little bee. It was a good thing there was no one coming!

One week I came in to work the bees and Dad asked me if I would drop him over in Illinois. He had bought an over-the-road bus and wanted to go pick it up. He was a welder for Parker Drilling, and his plan was to work all day on Friday. Then I was to pick him up at five and drive all night to Illinois. He drove all night, and we got there at eight the next morning. The family fixed us breakfast, and Dad got in the bus and started out driving all day through the foothills of Missouri. He got home sometime that night. He was up for forty-eight hours. I drove on into Arnold, Mo. which was only about four hours away.

In August of '79, we began to look for a position as a bus director. We had put out my resume to several places. I ended up with an interview in Fargo, North Dakota. We flew up for the weekend and stayed 'til Monday morning. They had nine buses that were bringing about three hundred kids. We talked, and something just did not feel right. I think the pastor felt the same way.

Chapter 9

MOVING TO DEL CITY

⸺⚬⚬⚬⸺

Pastor Brown had gotten a letter from a pastor in
Oklahoma City, asking him if he had a person
who could be his assistant pastor and run the bus
ministry. In August, we drove down for a weekend
to check the church out, but the pastor was not there,
and we were not able to meet with him. It was a
small church, running about a hundred. They had
two buses that were bringing in about twenty kids.
The interesting thing about this pastor was that I
had interviewed him in the early '70s when he was
in Rush Springs, Oklahoma. I was at the church in
Purcell when we had one bus, and my pastor, Wayne
Thompson, suggested that I go visit the church and
see how they were growing so fast. At that time they
were the fastest-growing church in our denomination.

They were running at least four hundred, with about five buses or so. I knew of the Pastor in Oklahoma City, and I really wanted to go there. Every time I tried to pin the pastor down about coming, he would put me off. I was afraid he would not hire me, but I kept praying. Finally he called and said okay. That pastor was Dale Gentry, who has written the forward to this book.

We moved to Del City and settled in. The Sunday before we got there, they had twenty-one on the two buses. The next week we had over seventy kids on those two buses, and everyone got so excited. Between '79 and '80 we grew to about 150 on three buses. We bought another bus from one of the other churches. It was called "Old Blue" because it had a terrible blue paint job. One bus was called "Green Bus," and the other one was orange. As the bus ministry grew, so did the church. By '81 we were running eight hundred and we were the fastest growing church in Oklahoma. The next bus I bought was on a closed bid at one of the schools. I saw this ad in the newspaper for a '72 Ford down in Eastern Oklahoma about 150 miles east of our church. I called to see if it was running, and the principal assured me that it was. So I sent down a bid of $400, thinking I could not go wrong with that bid. At least, I did not think I had anything to lose. In a few days, the principal called me and said I got the bus. I told him I would be down in a few days to get the bus. I had a guy go down with me, and he drove it back. We drove that bus around for a while and found that the brakes needed to be fixed. I took it to the shop and found that the brakes had never been touched and the shoes had cut right down into the drums. That little brake job cost us $1,400. Then we checked the front end, and it was totally worn out. To replace the kingpins, et cetera, was over $600. We also had to put several tires on it, which cost us another $400. Then we found the engine was drinking oil. So one of the men in the church said he would put in another engine for $600. This was a totally rebuilt engine. In the end, that was a very good bus.

Then we had a guy from a church in Arkansas who was taking a load of material down to Mexico to build churches. He had gotten almost to Oklahoma City when the engine in the bus he was driving blew. Their plan was to take the material down and give the bus to the church they were helping to build. For some reason he had called our church for help, and I got to talking to him about his project and felt we should help. This guy had taken off from his job for two weeks and needed to be back pretty soon. They told him that it would take $2,000 and a week to fix the engine. He had called his church, and they did not have the money to take care of the matter.

I prayed about what we should do. I called several men in the church and asked if we could give him the new bus that we had totally rebuilt. They felt we should do so. We had not driven the bus with that new engine, so I told the guy to take it easy for at least a hundred miles. We heard later that he made it down and got all the equipment there without any more trouble, but it is interesting how much money we had put into that bus and then be willing to send it to Mexico. I believe our church was blessed, because we were willing to help with that mission trip and the building of a new church. God works in funny ways. We thanked God that we had a bus that was ready for that kind of trip and duty. I am sure they used that bus for bringing kids to church.

After that there was an auction in one of the school districts. They had fifteen buses they were going to sell. I was very interested in seeing how they were going to sell. I got the okay to bid on up to $1,500. So I took a check with me. I bid on one bus and got it for $505. Then I got another for $425. Then the last one they said had a bad engine, so I got it for $285. I was still under my $1,500 limit, and everybody could not believe it. All these buses ran after we put batteries in them.

One Sunday we were having a big day, and Old Blue came in late. I was wondering what was taking it so long. Finally they came around the corner. That bus was just rocking, and it was totally dark inside. That bus was packed, with 107 kids on a forty-eight-passenger bus! I was so excited for the bus captain, but I was glad we did not get stopped by the police. We had two guys that made the 100 Club in 1981. We averaged about 300 kids on seven buses and three vans. God blessed us in many ways while we served as bus ministers.

Chapter 10

TRIP TO NEW MEXICO

—⊗⊗⊗—

In 1980 we were without a youth pastor, so I filled in. The young people had planned to go on a trip and had been raising funds for it. They had done several car washes and had gotten a little money. So when I started helping them, we sold each ticket for ten dollars for a wash and wax. These kids sold about a hundred tickets. I asked them how they were going to wash a hundred cars all in one day. It just so happened it rained the next Saturday, so we rescheduled for the next week. We only had about thirty cars show up, so we made out okay. We had talked about where to go, and I suggested Cloudcroft, New Mexico. I had been stationed at Holloman AFB, which was about thirty miles from Cloudcroft. I had gone up there many times and knew the area very well, so we made arrangements to go there. We found a place that had cabins that would house all forty-six of us. They had a large cabin with a kitchen, so the women could fix meals for the kids.

We had raised enough money for the cabins and fuel for the bus. We asked the church families if they would give us food, so we made a list of everything we needed. We got a wonderful response and were given four ice chests full of food. We had all the meals planned and knew about what we needed for each.

On a Sunday night we were to leave after we had done the radio broadcast on the JKIL. Pastor Gentry did one every Sunday night from ten to eleven, so we told everyone to be there by 11:30. It was in March, and it was still cold. Our church had an over-the-road 1956 Greyhound bus that eventually went over 400,000 miles. That bus had lost the air conditioning and heating system. Instead of fixing this system, someone had put in an electric generator system to power the two A/C units on top. There was no heating system, but we did have two little heating units that we took. They were not much help that night, because it got down into the teens and was freezing in that bus.

As we drove out of Oklahoma City, the wind started to blow out of the north at about forty miles per hour with a wind chill of zero degrees. Those heaters just could not keep up. At least we had some blankets and sleeping bags, and the kids made it okay. The front doors had very poor rubber seals around them, and that wind was coming in like crazy. I was sitting on the front seat to help our driver, and we were both in coats and gloves and were still freezing. There was no defroster on that bus, so the windows began to freeze over on the inside. I had to keep clearing the ice and fog off the window for the driver. That lasted until daylight, and we finally arrived in Hereford, Texas. That was our stop for breakfast. As we drove down the highway, we saw the restaurant on the other side of the street. Ray Savelle, our driver, pulled into a spot to turn around and go back. As he pulled down the street, there were these sloping curves that were pretty steep. As the bus got about halfway over the curve, it got stuck and would not move. We unloaded all the kids, and they walked back to the restaurant. Meanwhile, Ray was trying to figure out what to do. He finally called a wrecker to come out, lift the bus up and then drive it backward so we could go back out where we came in. I am not sure what that cost us; Ray took care of it. We got to the New Mexico border and we had to go through the inspection station. I had called ahead of time to make sure I had all the correct paperwork in order. The one thing they forgot to tell me was that we had to pay tax on our fuel, since it was a diesel. They held us up for about an hour while they called the state. They finally gave us a permit and charged us $75 in taxes for the fuel we had on board. They were not very nice about it, either. They wanted to charge us $300, but our driver talked them out of it. We drove on into New Mexico through Roswell and up into Ruidoso, which was very pretty with all the pine trees. As we were going up the mountain, we began to realize that the bus did not have much pulling power for hills and mountains.

We planned to stop at White Sands and play on the sand dunes for a couple of hours and then come back to town and have lunch. As we piled out of the bus and started for the dunes, the kids started climbing and sliding down them. A fifteen-year-old girl, Tammy Duke, hurt her ankle. We thought it might be broken, but she would not let us take her to the hospital to get it x-rayed. So her boyfriend, Rodney Moore, carried her everywhere they went for several days. That ankle turned black and blue, but it was not broken. Thank God. In that short two hours, most of the guys had taken their shirts off and, would you believe, gotten sunburned. Needless to say, they were very uncomfortable for several days. We went back to Alamogordo, New Mexico and stopped at Pizza Hut for lunch. Ray parked on a little hill and applied the emergency brake. As we were leaving, he forgot to release the brake. When we were about a mile out of town, the pastor came driving up beside us on the shoulder, honking and waving like crazy. I finally opened the door and heard him say that the bus was on fire. I looked back to see flames coming out of the back of the bus where the engine was! About that time, Ray realized the brake was still on and released it. He pulled over as quickly as he could, and I told everyone to unload. When I told them the bus was on fire, it was a mad rush for the door. Brian Moore was asleep when he heard that the bus was on fire. He jumped up and was the first one out of that bus. He ran, jumped a four-wire fence, and was about a hundred feet out in the field before looking around like ..."How did I get out here?" I asked him later, and he said he didn't know how he had gotten out there. After we thought about it, was kind of funny.

I had made sure we had all the emergency kits and the fire extinguisher. One issue was that fire extinguisher was right by the front door in a compartment, and this had to be opened. Every time I would try to open it, someone would bump into me on their way out. Someone finally let me get the fire extinguisher out, and I ran back to the rear of the bus while everybody told me to get back. I could not think of anything else but to get that fire out. We had been trained to operate those fire extinguishers in the service, so I knew what I was doing. I pulled the pin and squeezed the handle. The bus had fins on the sides where the flames were coming out, so I sprayed right in there. The flames died down and I opened the back and there was still a little fire. It was pretty clear that the brake had gotten too hot and the grease had caught fire. We inspected everything, and nothing was damaged. Ray had hit the kill switch in his panic. While trying to restart the bus, he forgot to say anything about it, or he just forgot that he had done so. I went back to the engine compartment and I reset it. The bus started right up. There was certainly some concern for a while.

We resumed our drive. We started up the mountain to Cloudcroft, New Mexico. It was nineteen miles to the top, and very steep. That bus did not have enough power to pull it up that mountain. We only had four forward gears and went down to second gear, so we were getting only ten miles per hour out of that bus. It took us two hours to get to the top. We unloaded everything into the cabins, and the ladies got to fixing dinner for the kids. That was on Monday night.

On Tuesday, the kids played games and ran around town. Wednesday night we were to go and minister at the Indian church across the mountain, about thirty miles away. At least, it was not back down the mountain. When we got there, we were not sure where the church was. I had been there several times, and there was always a sign that you could see coming up the mountain for the turnoff. That sign was turned to where we could not see it. I finally saw the sign just as we passed it. I told Ray that we could turn around down the road and come back. I had been down that road many times and knew there was not a turnoff for about five miles. Again, as he backed up the bus, he backed up too far, and the back wheels went down. We were stuck right across the highway. It was a very frightening situation, because the cars were coming from both directions, and it was dark. I was certainly afraid they were going to plow into us. We got all the boys out to help us push that bus. A lot of good that did. Ray finally got the bus to rocking and came over the hump. We determined then that the engine needed an overhaul. We all ran to get back on the bus and go on up to the church. We were about an hour late, but that did not seem to matter to them. They were just glad to have something new. We returned that night without any more problems.

The next day was Thursday. We had made plans for a snowmobile company to take us out to a canyon where there was still some snow. We rented twelve snowmobiles, and they brought them out for us to rent for about six hours. Those kids had never been on anything like that before. They turned us loose without any instruction, except to have fun. That was the wrong thing to do, because those kids went crazy on those machines. The first boy to get hurt was Keith Lewis. He had run the snowmobile up a hill as far as he could and then flipped it, hurting his arm. He got the machine turned back over and was riding it with one hand and the other one just hanging down. We did not find out 'til we got back that it was broken. We tried to get him to let us take him to the hospital, but he was having so much fun that he would not go.

The next one, Shawn, hit a tree stump and crashed her machine. I am sure she had a concussion. She did a job on that machine. The next boy crashed his machine, cutting his knee and lip. We took him to the hospital, and he got several stitches. He came back and wanted to ride some more! There was crash after crash, and those kids destroyed eight out of the twelve machines! The units were made of fiberglass, so they really looked bad. The owner was really upset and could not believe what he saw when he got back to pick up the machines. He wanted $1,200 for damages.

As the owner was loading the machines onto the trailer, the pastor and I were talking to him about the matter. One of his employees was driving one of the machines up the trailer and was supposed to stop, but the brakes did not work, and it came flying right over on top of us where we were standing. It knocked us both to the ground, with the machine on top of us. We were both hurt pretty badly. I thought it had broken my leg, but, thank goodness, it wasn't. Ray told the owner we were going to sue him for this accident. They finally settled on $400 for damages and let it go.

I know they were hopping mad over this, because I had another youth pastor tell me later that he had called to make arrangements to ride snowmobiles. The owner said he would take them out on the condition that they would follow the leader, stay in line, and not go over fifteen miles per hour. That youth pastor asked him why, and he began to tell the story about taking a youth group out to a canyon and turning them loose and how they destroyed most of his machines. He said he would never let that happen again.

We stayed 'til Friday night and were going to leave after dinner that night. We came down the mountain and around those curves at night. It was a little frightening, but I knew our driver could handle it. One of the ladies was so afraid we were going to run off the road that she began to praying very loudly. That was so distracting, I had to ask her to settle down. She just kept crying 'til we got off that mountain. I have heard that those kids still talk about that trip as being the best youth trip they had ever taken, even after thirty years.

We kept that bus for a while longer and took a trip to Washington, DC that summer in August. That trip was quite eventful as well. We had filled the gas tank up in DC, and it was about 900 miles back to Oklahoma City. Personally, I would have it filled up after about 400 to 500 miles, because the fuel gage wasn't working correctly. We got to Memphis, Tennessee, and I asked Ray, our driver, if we were going to get fuel. He felt like we could make it to Little Rock. I really felt we should stop and get fuel, but he just kept driving.

Well, wouldn't you know it, about halfway to Little Rock, that bus ran out of fuel. We were dead on I-40 and five miles from the nearest station. It was at least a hundred degrees outside, and the generator stopped working. It had gotten too hot and would not start. That bus, on the inside, was like an oven in no time. We had several older people on board, and I was really getting concerned for their health. Ray had gotten a ride to the station and came back with a five-gallon can of fuel. He put it in, but it still would not start. When you run a diesel engine out of fuel, you have to clean the filter and prime everything again. We did this several times and spent some time working on it with the help of the tow truck driver. Finally, he said, "Let me push you to the station." Before we could respond, he started pushing that bus and left us standing on the highway. I think there were three of us. Well, we thought that maybe that bus would start in just a little bit, and we could run and catch it. It finally started about a mile down the road … with big, black smoke coming out. Ray just kept going. The tow truck driver came back and picked us up. We will never forget about running out of fuel on the road home.

One time we let a youth group from Sallisaw, Oklahoma use that bus to go to Colorado for a ski trip. That was in January, and it was colder than cold. They drove to Liberal, Kansas and stopped for something to eat. They killed the bus without thinking, but should have left it running. Well, after one hour in zero-degree weather, that bus would not start. They kept trying 'til they burned the starter out. They called me at about two in the morning and asked what to do. I told them to get someone to push them 'til the bus started and not to kill it 'til they got to Colorado. We sold that bus after we got it back and had the starter rebuilt. We got $10,000 out of it, and the church was pretty happy because that is what they had paid for it.

We had gotten a handicap bus at an auction, and I thought I could get it fixed up to pick up people with wheelchairs, but I never could get it to work right and finally gave up and put it for sale in the newspaper. There was a guy who called about it who had a '73 Ranch Arrow Ford. He said it had a new engine in it, and he wanted to make a trade. I was asking $3,500 for the bus. We got to talking, and then we took the car and he gave us $1,800 in cash.

Our principal, Jim Howard, drove that car for many years after that. We used that as a pickup for just about everything around the church and school.

During that time our pastor had gone down to Jamaica to preach and see some of our missionaries. One of our missionaries took him up to one of the mountains to show him what one of the missionary's pastors had done. He would walk ten miles up the mountain and dig the foundation for a new church. He did this day after day 'til he got it done. He had no money to buy concrete but believed that God would give him the money to build the church. Then Pastor Gentry met him. He told him that God told him to dig the footing and someone would come and see the need. God spoke to Pastor Gentry to come back and raise the money to build that church. There was another pastor that had a real need for a bus. Pastor got back asked me if we could give him one of our buses. I was concerned, because I did not think we had a bus that was good enough to drive to Florida and then ship down to Jamaica. It just so happened that I was looking in the paper again and found a man that wanted to sell his bus. I called him and was talking to him about the bus and all the things he had done to it. He said he had had a heart attack and wasn't able to travel like he wanted to. He had rebuilt the engine and transmission. He had put new brakes and tires on it. I went to look at the bus, and it was just what I was looking for. We bought the bus for $1,800 and told the man what we were going to do with it. He just cried and felt very blessed.

Now the story of that bus is very interesting. When I got the bus, we started to tell people that we were going to send it to Jamaica. We had a young couple who started attending our church. The husband's name was Jim Burns. He was a very tall man, about six foot eight and as thin as a bean pole. He had gotten saved after having some run-ins with the law. Jim and his wife were willing to drive the bus to Florida and load it onto a ship. We knew it would take $2,000 to ship it down there, so we raised that amount. We loaded it with clothes and two motorcycles. I had made all the arrangements to load the bus onboard the ship, and everything went fine up to that point. But when it got to port in Jamaica, that was a different story. Customs there required the church to pay over $2,000 to release the bus. I did not find this out until later, but some way the church was able to raise the money.

That church was so excited to get that bus. They put seats in it and used it almost every day. When we went down to Jamaica to dedicate the church on the mountain, they let us use that bus. The first night, the driver ran out of gas and we had to wait on a five-gallon can of gas that cost about twenty-five dollars down there. Gas was five dollars per gallon. We were about an hour late for the service that night, but that did not matter to them. They were glad to see us. The next night, one of our drivers had to drive the bus up the hill. That road was very narrow and filled with lots of curves. We were all glad to get back on the bus at about midnight and start down the hill. As we were going down the hill, the driver said the brakes were getting very hard, and he could not slow the bus down. I told him to shift down quickly to slow the bus down. I thought we were going to drop the transmission, but it helped slow it down. Then he used the emergency brake, and we made it down. Those hairpin turns were a little frightening, and we had a lot of people praying. We found the brake booster had gone out. When we got back to the states, I located a rebuilt bus for $600 and had it flown down. Customs got us again for $300.

From '79 to '82 I was having more and more trouble seeing, especially at night. I got to where I could not find the queen bee when I checked my beehives. We moved those bees at night, and the driving really got to me. On one occasion Dad and I were moving two loads of bees from one location to another. I was following Dad in my truck, and we were going downhill. The trailer started pushing me, so I tried slowing it down by shifting down. About halfway down, I heard this huge crack of lightning. It hit right in front of me, and I about jumped right out of my seat. I was shaking all over. When that lightning hit, everything just became very bright, and then I could not see the road or the white line. I was totally horrified. That was one of the last moves I made with those bees. I sold them and got out of the business.

Another time, the pastor and I decided to drive up to Davenport to a pastors' conference. We called the wives to tell them we were going at the last minute. So after the radio broadcast, we left. Now Pastor started to drive and about an hour out got very sleepy and asked me to drive. Betty, my wife, was sitting in the front seat with me and would tell me when I needed to move over to the right or left. At that time I don't think Pastor Gentry really knew that I was having trouble seeing. I was considered blind from the service. I believed I could still do it.

Well, I can tell you that I had several close calls. I was driving around on a bus route one Saturday. To my left, a kid came flying down the hill on his bike, and I hit him. I never saw him. It wrecked his bike. I was going slow enough that he was not hurt. His dad was sure upset at him. I bought him a new bike. Another time I was going over to the church at an early hour, and it was still dark. As I drove along the street that had no markings, I heard a crash and stopped quickly and went around the right side. On the ground was a teenage girl and her bike. Somehow she had gotten into my path, or I had gotten into her path. Her bike was a mess. She was not hurt, but I took her home. She told me that was her new bike and it was the first time she decided to ride her bike to school. She was pretty upset. I never heard whether the insurance company had to pay them anything. One night I had to go over to get something at the store, and I turned right into a big highline post, messing up the left fender. In about a six-month period I wrecked my pickup three times. I also wrecked one of our cars. My insurance canceled me, and I decided it was time to stop driving before I killed someone. That was the hardest thing to give up, that independence.

In 1981 we started a Christian school. We started with seventy-eight students, ranging from kindergarten to eighth grade. That was very good for the first year. I was over the school the first year, and the lady under me was a very interesting person. She had taught in the public school system and wanted to run the school the way she saw fit. We finally let her go and started to look for someone who could do a better job. That is when we found Jim and Diana Howard. They had been teaching back east and wanted to come back to Oklahoma because of family. So we hired them. I helped the pastor locate several other couples for the school and church. We hired three of those couples, and they became great assets to the school. As of this writing, the Howards are still there, and Ms. Ditto is still doing books for the school, even after thirty years.

Back in '84 we had agreed to buy the five acres behind the church for $70,000, with a down payment of $16,000. It was the property of one of the Baptist churches that was trying to build a church out on the interstate highway. Then they wanted it back to sell it for a higher price. Someone had told them it was worth over $200,000 and that they should just give us our money back and sell it at the higher price. So that is what they did. They broke the contract and returned our $16,000. Now, that really upset the pastor and the board (I served on the school board for seven years, from '81 to '88). The pastor had called a board meeting to discuss what we should do about suing the Baptist church for breach of contract. They took a vote, and all the members voted to sue the Baptist church, except me. I did not agree, and I am so grateful that God gave me the boldness to stand up and tell them that we should not sue. The first thing everyone wanted to know was why I felt like we should not sue. The Bible tells us not to take people to court unless we have to. Well, I expressed that to them, and they understood. Then I said this: "If God wants us to have that property, they will not be able to sell it, and it will come back to us." I also told them that if they sued, the whole matter would go public, and it would hurt both churches. So they rescinded the vote to sue and took the $16,000 back.

Well, would you believe, the very next year they came back to us and asked us if we still wanted the five acres, and, if so, we could still have it for the $70,000 that was on the first contract. Well, that time around we did not wait. We went and got a loan and gave them the money before they could back out again. The school now has a football and baseball field on that property. That school grew from seventy-eight students in 1981 to over five hundred.

Chapter 11

INVESTMENT AND GOING BROKE

—∞∞∞—

I n 1982, I thought I would try real estate. I went to
real estate classes for several weeks and got my
real estate license. I also had an insurance license
in that area. I had bought several houses and rented
them out. I thought I was doing very well; I hit the
millionaire club and made some good money. But
then came '83 and '84. The interest rate went up to
21 percent, and the housing market went down the
tubes. At the beginning of June 1983, I had twen-
ty-eight houses on the board that I had either listed or
sold. By the end of that same month, fifteen of them
fell out. Then in '84 and '85, the oil business dried
up in the United States. Oklahoma lost over 100,000
jobs, and many people left the state looking for work

in other places. I had nine rental houses and had only three that were occupied. I started trying to sell the properties. They were not worth what I had paid for them two years before. I had mortgaged our home to buy the rental houses. I had no income coming in on anything, so I got behind on the house payments. The mortgage company would not talk to me about a refinance unless I could catch up on the back payments. The worst part was that I had sold a piece of property on a contract to a guy, and he let it go back. I had sold the contract that I had but did not read the fine print. So they were also suing me. I was deep in debt and could not see any way out, so in 1985 we had to declare bankruptcy. The hardest thing I ever did was to stand before the judge and tell him why I could not pay my debts. I hope I never have to go through that again. I was depressed to no end.

What I did learn in all that was that family means everything. My wife stayed with me even though we lost our home. Sure, we all make mistakes and have to learn our lessons over again. I heard this from Zig Ziglar: "The person that doesn't make any mistakes is dead, and the only one that lived that did not make any mistakes was Jesus Christ." We all make mistakes, and we have to learn from them and go on.

Chapter 12

GETTING FIRED

—⁂—

From '84 to '87, I was working at the church and drawing a small check. I was over the bus ministry and seniors and singles. We had changed pastors in 1985, and there were a lot of financial problems in the church. A lot of people had moved to other places for jobs, so we were down in numbers. The bus ministry heyday was over, and we only had three buses running on routes. On the last day of 1986, the pastor took me out to lunch and told me that he was going to lay me off. That was one of the hardest things that ever happened to me. I had never been let go from a job. It was always my choice, and that really got to me. I was depressed for some time.

Our son, Robbie, had been doing a paper route for the Dallas Morning News, plus he was going to school. So I started to help him. We would get up at two in the morning and go and pick up papers and work till about five or six, depending on what time the papers came in from Dallas. Then I would sleep most of the day. I would pray, and nothing would happen.

I had gone to school and gotten a Masters in Education. I had several interviews, but nothing was working. I had my resume out to several places, and I would pray, "Lord, send me anywhere but California." I prayed that for about a year and a half, and nothing happened. It was like God was not around, and I could not hear from Him. I was able to sell some foreclosures to make ends meet. With the paper route, we did okay.

Chapter 13

ELEMENTARY
SCHOOL PRINCIPAL

—⸙—

About June of '88, I was praying, and God impressed on me that the reason that nothing had opened up was that I had put too many restrictions on Him about where I would go. I fell on my face and prayed, "Okay, God, anywhere." Just about that time, a pastor called me from El Cajon, California. He asked me if I would come and be the principal for his school. He told me that one of his deacons was on a fishing trip in Texas and would like to drive up and interview me, so we met at a Denny's on I-35. I guess it went okay, because after he got back, they called me for another interview and asked me if we would come.

So we began to make plans to move to California. Now we had lived in Oklahoma for the last twenty years, except for the year we were in training at the church in Arnold, Missouri. Our whole family was there, and we really did not know anyone in California, But we felt it was the door that God had opened and that we must step through that door and make the move. When you are trying to do God's will, sometimes it is hard for people and families to understand why we do certain things. I think Mom and Dad somewhat understood us, because he had quit a really good job at Caterpillar in Oklahoma and moved down to Smithville, Oklahoma to pastor a small church. Dad pastored thirteen different churches over a forty-five-year period. Some he pastored more than once. Most of the churches were around the Purcell area, within the thirty-mile zone. So for him to give up his good job and go down to Smithville was hard to understand at that time. Dad had always worked full time as a welder after he stopped sharecropping in '59. He was a welder by trade and never had a problem getting a job. So for that move, he was able to go to work on another dam at De Queen, Arkansas.

I think Betty's family hated to see us go. We had lived in Del City for nine years and had a lot of friends we hated to leave. We had been renting a place for about two years, since we had lost the home in '86. We had a pretty house that was about 1,800 square feet with a pool. We rented that for about $650 per month. We had a lot of furniture and knew we could not get it all in a truck, so we had a great big garage sale. We were able to sell several things and hoped that it would be enough. We left on August 5, 1988.

We rented a twenty-six-foot truck from Budget. It was a diesel and could run about seventy miles per hour on level ground, but on those hills it would get down to thirty miles per hour. Robbie, our eldest son, drove the rental truck, and James, our youngest, rode with him. Betty drove the pickup, pulling a trailer with the car on it. We were loaded down. It took us three days to get there. The last day, we stopped in El Centro to get lunch. As we opened the door, we were met with heat like I had never felt before. It was at least 115 degrees. We had our dog, Max, with us, and I decided to stay with him while the rest went in to eat. I thought we both were going to die in that heat. During the next two hours we were in for it, because we had to drive out of that valley and up the mountain. The pickup started to overheat with the air conditioner running, so we turned that off and rolled down the windows. We were met with a blast of heat. The pickup continued to get hotter, so then we had to turn the heater on to cool the engine. It worked, but Betty and the dog and I were cooked. I was never so glad to get to the top of that mountain.

We had depended on the pastor to rent a house for us, and he found one for $800. It was a small house without air conditioning. El Cajon usually has a very mild summer with a temperature of around seventy-six degrees during summer, but that Labor Day weekend the Santa Ana winds started blowing and the temperature went up to 110 degrees in the box (el cajon means "the box"). The heat was just terrible.

On Saturday, the pastor's daughter was to be married in the church at two in the afternoon. Both air conditioners were down, and it began to get very hot in the church. They had a beautiful cake, but the icing began to melt and run and it was a mess. The wind was blowing seventy to eighty miles per hour, and it took part of the roof off the school building.

On Sunday, we drove down to the beach to see if we could find a cold place to eat and hang out.

I think everybody else had the same idea, because you could not find a parking place. We finally found somewhere to park and eat lunch. Then we went out on the pier. It was still 95 degrees, with the wind blowing out of the east. That was a very interesting weekend. It lasted four days, and we thanked God that no fires broke out in that area. When those winds get that strong and come out of the east in California, fires are sure to follow.

After we were there about two months, our son, Robbie, joined the Army. That was a big hole in our hearts.

I jumped on the school budget to see where we were. Now, most church schools run on a shoe-string budget, and El Cajon Christian School was no exception. I had reviewed the budget for about two months, and as I reviewed it, I saw some areas that were not helping it. Part of the pastor's salary came out of the school budget, and the church secretary was also paid from that budget, plus all the utilities. I took these findings to the pastor and told him that he could not afford to pay my salary. He said, "That is why I hired you—to figure out what we need to do." I suggested that we do some fundraising, so we did about three that fall. The other thing I suggested was to start a preschool, which they had never had. We had to make some adjustments to the school, like adding some bathrooms in one of the rooms. By March 1, we opened with about thirty-five students, and it grew to about a hundred students by the time we left in November of '90.

After I had been there for about three months, I was in the pastor's office and we were having our weekly talk. For some reason he asked me to plug in a TV. The outlet was right beside me. He handed me the cord, and I was feeling all around to figure out where to plug it in. I can still hear the words, "Are you blind?" I looked at him and said, "Yes, I am." He fell back in his chair and said, "What, are you blind?" That was the first time I had told anyone in California that I was blind. I know that hit our pastor like a brick. Now, the question has always been ... should I have been upfront with him at the very beginning? I don't know. I was not using a cane, and I could get around pretty good. I found out later that some of the staff would see me run into things, and they thought I was drinking. I can assure you that I never drank in my life. I guess I thought they might have figured it out when they never saw me driving. Betty, my wife, and the boys were always the ones driving.

I was able to get reinstated as a minister with the Assembly of God in 1989. I had let it lapse. I was also having a lot of trouble seeing at that time. I had gotten acquainted with the guy who was doing a fundraiser with us. Come to find out he was employed by the VA. I got to talking with him about my condition. He said he had filed claims for veterans. He did some research on my case and found that I could be upgraded to a higher rate than I was getting. This became total and permanent.

While the eye doctor was confirming that I was almost totally blind, he asked me if I had heard about the Blind Center for Veterans and if I knew who the VIST coordinator was. I had heard of neither, so he took me right over and introduced me to the lady. She started telling me about all the things that were available for blind veterans. I was in shock. That is the way most of our veterans react when they find out that there is something that will really help those of us who are blind. She put me in for going to the blind center in June of '91. My time in El Cajon was a real learning experience, and I am grateful for the opportunity to serve as principal for that time.

Chapter 14

BACKSIDE
OF THE DESERT

———&&&———

G od had been dealing with me to pastor a church, and I was willing to go anywhere. So one day we made an appointment with the district superintendent, and he was telling us about a small church out in the Salton Sea area that really needed a pastor. We decide to go and try out. I really did not feel that I had done very well that weekend. I told the Pastor I did not think they wanted me, but he said, "That is not what I heard." I was really feeling the pressure of going back again. I think they would have taken anyone who would come out and stay in the area. Most of the pastors, up 'til then, had lived at least fifty miles away or more. So we decided to move out. Each Saturday we would load up the pickup and move a little at a time. We put our things in one of the rooms in the church. We would stay all night in the church, where there was a couch that we made into a bed, a bathroom with a tub, and a kitchen. We were waiting for one of the ladies in the church who was going to move and wanted to rent her house to us.

From October 1990 'til August of '94, I served as pastor in Salton City, California. The church was called the West Shores Assembly of God. I put in for some other churches, and this is one that would take me. I really think it was because they did not have a lot of choices. They had no money to pay a pastor, and no housing. There were not many people who could afford to move to the area and pastor without any jobs available.

The first time we drove out to Salton City to preach, we had to drive over the mountain to El Centro. We then had to leave the comfort of El Cajon, at about 76 degrees. We went over the mountain, and when we got to the bottom of the mountain we asked ourselves, "What have we done?" In October, the weather in Salton City was still a hundred degrees! Well, we drove up to Salton city and drove right through the town, without ever seeing the town. The church was right on the highway, but we never saw it that first time we came through. At that time, Salton City was thirty-six square miles with about six hundred people living there. The town had a community center; a bank; a store where you could get gas, mail, and a few items like milk and bread; and about three joints where you could get a hamburger.

The church board consisted of two eighty-five-year-old men and one seventy-one-year-old man. The church needed a lot of work. They had started to put in a handicapped bathroom. They had a big dirt pile in the middle of the hallway with a long ditch that went about thirty feet. For the next three months, we worked very hard to get all this finished so we could dedicate the church. They had started the church in '87, and that was three years later. Those eighty-five-year-old men flat worked me under the bench. It was amazing how hard these guys worked. So in March of '91 we were able to dedicate that church building.

The interesting thing was that our son, James, went away to college in August of '90. At that time, we were still living in El Cajon, and it was very nice. That following fall we moved to Salton City, California, to pastor. So James came home in December for Christmas break. He was supposed to come in at nine in the evening from Denver, but the snow was so bad that the plane was delayed. He did not get in until four in the morning, so we stopped for breakfast and started on our way over the hill and down into the desert. We came to the drop-off into Borrego Springs, California. From that point on, all you could see was desert for miles and miles. We said to James, "You see that water way out there? That is where we live."

I know he was in disbelief that we had moved way out there to no-man's-land. He started asking us where all the pizza places and shopping malls were. We just looked at him and smiled and said, "Well, you go thirty-five miles to the south and thirty-five miles to the north, and you can find the pizza place or go shopping." He could not wait to go back to college.

Our son, Robbie, was in the Army in Germany during the first Gulf War. We thought he would not have to go to the Gulf, but the first thing we heard was that they were sending the First Armored Division over. I'm not sure when he got there, but he was in the group that crossed in behind the Republican Guard. We were very concerned. He had told us that he was in combat engineers, and the tank that he commanded was a mine clearer with two thousand pounds of TNT to fire the equipment to clear minefields. We found out later that he had some close calls.

In May of '91 the VA called me to go to the Blind Rehab Center in Palo Alto, California. We left the first of June, just when the weather was getting really hot. I left my wife and our son, James, who had come for the summer, in charge of the church. I went up to the Blind Center. It was like a light had been turned on. I got a CCTV to enlarge print and reverse its color. You would have a black background with white letters. That really helped me to read and study the Bible. I made it my goal to read the Bible through for the rest of the year.

During that time, I also learned to always carry my white cane to keep from running over people. I learned several other skills and got to visit several San Francisco sights, like the Golden Gate Bridge, Alcatraz, Liberty Ship, Half Moon Bay, the red oak trees, and rodeos. We were also blessed to get to go Candlestick Park in late June. That was one of the coldest days I can remember up there. The wind was blowing off the bay, and it was downright cold. I had on an extra shirt, a sweatshirt, and a coat, and I still froze.

In August, Betty and the boys came up to see me. Robbie had got a vacation after they got back from Germany. His future wife, Tracy, also came out. So they drove up and spent a week touring the area. They also wanted to go to one of the ball games at Candlestick Park. It was August and, would you believe, it was so hot and humid you could just be sitting and start sweating.

I got to go home about the middle of August. It was over 115 degrees, and I was not ready for that heat. Betty and James rubbed it in and said, "Now see what we have been putting up with all summer. You run off to school and leave us here to suffer this heat while you are up there in the cold weather."

Well, would you know it, two weeks after we got home, the air conditioner went out. It was 117 degrees. It was so hot in the house that we could not sleep. It was a good thing we had a pool. We would stay in it 'til about midnight and then try and get some sleep. The owner did not want to fix the air conditioner, so I had it fixed. It cost the same amount that was due for rent. I just sent them the paid bill in place of the rent. They did not like that at all and asked us to move. One of the ladies in the church had two houses and was finishing up the new one and wanted to sell the older home. She offered it to us for $65,000 and was willing to carry the loan. We thought that would be a good buy at the time.

We moved into the house in October of '91. We knew it had some problems but thought nothing about it. The winter of '93 brought a lot of rain. The normal amount per year out there is two inches, but that winter it rained at least seven inches. The water began to impact the west side of the house and was not draining away from it like it should. We tried to drain the water around the house, but it would not drain right. When it began to dry up, that clay started to swell up and raise the corner of the house, all along the west side. Before we knew it, we had a house that was nine inches higher on the west side and the foundation had cracked all along that side. We had earthquake insurance, so I called them. They spent half a day taking measurements and dirt samples. Now the reason I had called them was that on June 28, 1992, there was an earthquake called the "Big Bear" quake. It was a 7.5 on the Richter scale. I thought that might have caused part of the damage.

But the report came back as earth movement, and they were not going to pay anything. I called a contractor to come out and give us some estimates of what it was going to take to fix the problems. That estimate was $65,000. They would have to jack the whole house up and put pillows about eight feet down. Then they would set the house back down. Well, that was too much for me.

We had also put in a pool, and that pool began to rise up on the west side and started to crack. They said all that was from the earth movement from the rains and from the watering I was doing. One of the guys talked me into trying to grow some palm trees. I planted about 1,500 seeds, not expecting all of them to come up, but I think every one of them came up. I had been watering them on a regular basis and, I guess, the water made the clay swell. Before I knew it, the pool rose by five inches on the west side and cracked in several places. I had to sue the pool company, and it took four years to get any money back.

On the bright side, the people from the church were so kind and seemed very thankful someone would move way out there to pastor their church. It certainly did not matter that I was blind, because many of them were dealing with all kinds of physical problems. We saw many of our people go on to be with the Lord. We celebrate their dying, because they were in a better place with no more pain. Thank God.

Both trustees that were eighty-five died while we were there. We went to the hospital on many occasions to see the sick. During that time we put over 150,000 miles on several vehicles.

While our son was in the Army, he was stationed in Germany for three years and left his truck with us. For about two years, Betty drove it. On one occasion, one of the sisters from the church called and said they were taking her husband to the hospital and she needed a ride. She did not think that he was going to make it. We picked her up and drove to the hospital that night. Well, would you know it, that guy started feeling better and was ready to go home in about five hours. So they discharged him. We only had the truck and could only get three people in the cab. Those people were on the larger size. I was only about 150 pounds, but there was still no room for me in the cab. Now, mind you, it was only twenty degrees outside. We talked it over, and I decided to ride in the back. It was an open bed, so I knew it was going to be very cold. We asked the nurse if they could help, and she gave me two big trash bags and two blankets. I put the blankets around me and rolled up in them. Then I put the trash bags on the outside as best as I could and lay down in the bed of the

157

truck. I lay crossways right up against the cab, trying to stay out of the wind. Boy, did I get cold. That was one of the longest thirty-five miles I have ever been on. Every time we hit a bump in the road, I could feel it. I was afraid someone might think that I was trying to get a free ride.

Another time, we were having a dinner party for the church, and this lady named Bonnie just passed out and died right in front of me. We called 911. The ambulance was already making a run north to the hospital that was about forty-five miles away. For the next thirty minutes, we did CPR on her while waiting for the ambulance to arrive. Unfortunately, the ambulance had been broken into and all the equipment had been stolen. There was nothing they could do to revive her, so they just picked her up and took her to the hospital where they pronounced her dead on arrival.

On another occasion they called me to come quickly, because one of the men just had a stroke. We rushed to his side and saw that the man looked like he was dead. His eyes had rolled back into his head, and he was not breathing very well. I had taken a bottle of olive oil to anoint him with. I put some on my finger and began to pray. Well, I had forgotten to put the cap back on the bottle. I had it in my left hand and had my right hand on his head. As I was praying, unbeknownst to me, I started pouring the oil on his right side where he was paralyzed. I prayed probably about ten minutes. Now, mind you, this guy had been unconscious. In a few minutes he began moving around. His color came back, and he began to breathe more normally. During the twenty-five minutes of waiting for the ambulance, he began to speak some words, and by the time those guys got the gurney into the room, he was talking normal. The medical tech asked him if he could get up. He got right off that bed and onto the other, with a little help, of course. We were all amazed at what God had done.

His wife told me later that the right side had been affected by the stroke, and all the area where the oil went had been healed. The doctors were all amazed when he did get to the hospital. They could tell he had a stroke. He stayed a few days and then went home. After questioning him, we found out that while I was praying and the oil was going down his right side, he said it was like the hand of God touching him.

Chapter 15

DIVINE APPOINTMENT

———— ∽∂∞∂∽ ————

In 1978, we were in Arnold, Missouri, training for the ministry. There we met several students who we were able to help get placed. One of those was Larry Key. He was a young man of seventeen when he came to the church to be trained. He could hardly read and had gotten saved after having a drinking binge. He really stood out in my mind at the time. The first day he came in he had long hair and was pretty wild. Pastor Brown took care of that pretty quickly and had his hair cut really short. He had many long talks with him over several weeks, and he became a very good student with the help of his future wife.

When I went to Del City First Assembly in '79, my pastor thought we did a great job and started telling all his pastor friends about the school in Arnold, Missouri. He told Pastor Shafer in Altus, Oklahoma. Pastor Shafer called me one day and asked me who would make a good youth pastor for his church. He was expanding his ministry and wanted someone who would work hard. I suggested Larry Key and Randy Wick. He interviewed and brought them both to Altus, and I believe they stayed about two years. Larry went back to St. Louis and started his own church, and for the next ten years made a number of trips to Mexico on mission trips. He would take work crews to work on church buildings and school projects. He really had a heart for missions.

In '92 I had a group from Phoenix, Arizona, come help us with some outreach. We put them up in homes, and from Wednesday to Friday we would knock on doors in our community and in the other two towns on the west shores of the Salton Sea. I wanted them to stay the weekend, but they were unable to do so. They suggested that a friend of theirs come and minister. I said, "Okay. What is his name, and do you have a phone number?" They told me his name was Larry Key! Now I had not heard from Larry since about '84, so I had no idea where he was or what he was doing at the time. I asked, "Is he from

Missouri?" and they said, "Yes." I asked if his wife was Ronda. It was. I said, "I know this guy." I got on the phone and started talking with him, and it was just like old times.

He came out that weekend to minister. I asked him what he was doing in Phoenix and he said he wanted to go into Mexico and minister on a regular basis, but he had no connections yet. We invited him back for a weeklong revival. I invited the Hopeville church to come over to help us with the music. I knew Steve, the pastor, because we had followed him in El Cajon as principal of the school. He played the piano, and they sang. I knew that would be of great help to our church and the revival. Well, that Monday evening, Steve brought some of his church to help. One of the ladies who came was a dentist in Hopeville, and we began talking with her. She shared that she was from Mexico. Not only that, her uncle was the bishop for a number of churches in Mexico. Larry began to share his vision of wanting to minister in Mexico. She said, "Let me talk with my uncle tomorrow, and I will call you." She was able to set up a meeting with her uncle in Mexico for Thursday, so we drove over with them. What an open door that was. He invited Larry to his church the very next weekend.

After that one meeting the doors opened wide, and Larry was always driving down to Mexico. I feel like I had a part in helping Larry get connected down there. He ended up moving his family down to Calexico to be right across to border from Mexicali, where he was doing most of his ministering. They had been renting a house down there. Someone gave them $10,000 to put down for a house of their own. Larry called me one day and told me that nobody wanted to work with him because they did not feel he could make the payments. I suggested he contact a friend of ours who we knew was in the real estate and mortgage business. His name was Daryl Igegnrom. I called Daryl about Larry and gave him the information, and he was able to help them buy a house. They lived there a number of years, ministering in Mexico, the US, and the Philippines. Larry helped raise funds to build several churches in Mexico, and he did a great job down there.

In about 1999, Larry was doing a lot of ministering in the Philippines and was gone a lot. It was getting difficult to get out of that part of California to catch a plane, so he felt they should move back to Phoenix, where it was much easier to catch a plane. He was also ministering a lot in Phoenix to raise funds to go overseas. They were able to sell their house in Calexico and even cleared some pretty good money. He called me one day and said they had purchased a nice home in Phoenix with their down payment. What a blessing.

Chapter 16

FROM HELL TO HEAVEN

———❦———

In '94 I felt like it was time to move again, pastor, and have a school. I wanted a place where I could use my administration skills. We began to pray that God would open a door for us to move somewhere. We would pray for anyplace but Los Angeles. If you recall, when we were in LA in '76, I never wanted to live in that place. So, naturally, that was the way I was praying. Well, I was getting serious with God one day when he spoke to me and asked me why I didn't want to go to LA. God wanted me down in the LA area, so I finally said, "Okay, anywhere, God."

We had a friend, Jerry, from the desert who was in Gardena, California. One day I noticed that he had resigned from the church. So I picked up the phone and called him. He said that, yes, he had resigned and it was effective on August 14. Now this was in June that the notice had come out. He told me about all the trouble he was having with the board. He was only in his thirties and had been a youth pastor in El Cajon at the same time I was in El Cajon as a principal. He had pastored once before going to Gardena as pastor.

The thing that was troubling Jerry was that they were unable to make the building payments for the church and that enrollment had dropped off at the school. They were doing the best they could. I decided to send up my resume, and they called me in July for an interview.

The first thing one of the deacons told me when he saw my white cane was, "I did not know we were going to interview a blind guy." I thought to myself, "What has he got against blind people?" The interview went well. They called me to preach one weekend in July of '94. I was elected to come and be their pastor.

The board wanted me to just pastor the church, but the school was having a lot of problems. I knew that if something did not happen at the school to get the enrollment up, there would not be a church or school. I looked at the books and the finances and knew there was no way that the payments and salaries could be met with the income that was coming in.

One of the first things the area director said to me was, "Will you make sure you make the building payment before you take a paycheck?" He asked me if I had other income, which I did, from the VA compensation.

I jumped into that school with both feet, and we were able to get the enrollment up by thirty or so students, which really helped our income. We had a few new people come to the church also. It seemed like everything was going well until one day the board demanded to see the books and had their own meeting without me. I had been giving them a monthly report of what was coming in and going out, but for some reason they did not believe the reports. They seemed to be upset that we had gotten things to go well for the school even though I had not put one of the board members in charge of the school, which was what he wanted. It seemed that we were having a real battle. It became difficult to preach. The one board member had an adult Sunday school class, and he would often run over past the time for the service to start. I had to talk with him about it, and it just did not matter. Anyway, I would start the service on time, even with just a few people. In November '94 they were talking behind my back and even went to the district to get me out. When the one board member brought in a lady who was seeing angels and calling up the dead, that was it for me. I called the district representative and told them what was going on. The final word was that the district asked the board to resign. They did so and took fourteen people with them. The next Sunday we had nineteen in church and never looked back after that.

I think the board thought that since I was blind I would not be able to take care of things and they would still be in charge. In a lot of churches, the board members dominate the pastor and tell him what to do and how high to jump. Plus they will tell him what he can preach. This is very wrong, because God sets a pastor in place, and he hears from God what to preach. Often board members do not know how to come under the authority of the pastor, and, therefore, you have this conflict that is not healthy for the church. Board members must come under authority or go on down the road. It is said churches all need a bowel movement. I heard that from an old-time preacher, and I believe he knew what he was talking about!

With the right tools, A blind person can do anything anybody else can do. Never doubt a blind person. They will try harder and will even work longer to get the job done. That first year we did miss a few paychecks, but overall we begin to climb back out of the red. We were able to sign up for a few of the state programs for the preschool, and that expanded our income base. The reason I call this "From Hell to Heaven" is that in the desert it would get up to 120 during the summer. That would go on from March to October. Then the hot wind would blow with sand so thick that you could hardly see across the street. Now, in Gardena the weather was so perfectly nice that we did not have to use the air conditioner very often. At about four in the afternoon, the marine layer would come in, and it would feel like the air conditioner came on. We could have flowers and a garden year round, which was very nice. We tried to grow tomatoes and some other vegetables out in the desert, but they would just burn up. The only things I could grow out there were palm trees. Those things would grow like crazy.

In January of '95 our son James arrived to help us with the church. He and Julie had gotten married in August of '94, and they both had teaching degrees.

She started teaching at the public school, and James was in charge of the children and youth at the church and was also teaching the third grade at our school.

It was like starting over with a new church. After all those other people left, we just started rebuilding the church with new people. We had one couple that stayed with us and began to help us with the finances in the school and church. Steve would come by early in the morning and work for a couple of hours, and then go to his job at an auto parts place. He was very good at looking at the reports and telling what was going on in the accounts. We set up a new accounting system, and he was able to see to several unpaid accounts. It just took a little follow-up to get these accounts brought up to date. After about a year and a half, I asked Steve if he would come on staff. At that time he was out of work. He agreed and became a very valuable asset to the school and church.

Chapter 17

30TH ANNIVERSARY

———∞∞∞———

I n 1997 it was our thirtieth anniversary. I wanted
to do something very special. We had gotten a
flier from one of the senior groups that was plan-
ning a cruise up the inside pathway to Alaska. It was
to be a seven-day trip. We were to fly from LAX to
Vancouver, Canada. From there we were to get on
a Holland America ship on a Saturday between two
and five in the afternoon. We made it with plenty of
time. This was our first time to be on one of those big
ships. It is hard to believe how big those things are.
I believe this one was about 1,000 feet long with ten
or eleven decks. We were three decks down. Instead
of taking an elevator, Betty made us take the stairs
all the time.

That first night, early in the morning, we noticed the ship was really going up and down, and on Sunday morning we were all getting seasick. We asked what was going on. They told us that we were having to go through a storm and that the water was a little rough. They passed out medicine for nausea and told everyone to go up to the outside deck and get in the center of the ship where it would not be as rough. They were right about that, and by noon we had gotten through that storm.

On Monday we docked at Juneau, Alaska. It was a very interesting place for the capital. There was a lot of history. Tuesday we were to dock at Skagway. We took the train up the mountain to the place where you cross over to the Yukon. I cannot fathom how those gold miners were able to get 1,500 pounds of supplies up that mountain. There was one place with at least a thousand foot drop-off where, they say, thousands of horses, dogs, and men died. All the time Betty was outside taking pictures, I was sitting inside. She said she saw some mountain sheep way over on another hill. We finally got to the top, and they moved the engine from the front to the back, which took a little while. At least the brakes did not go out going down. I would not want to be on that train if the brakes ever went out.

The next day we went to another town and we just walked around. Then on Thursday we went to the glacier. Some got off the ship and took a helicopter ride over the top of the glacier. When the ice falls off, it is called calving. It was so cold on the deck that I went back to the room while Betty stayed out and took pictures with our movie camera.

One thing about a cruise is that you will not get hungry, because there is something open at all times where you can get food. We came back down to Vancouver, Canada by Saturday morning. We unloaded, and from there we took buses down to Seattle, Washington. We made our connection by just a few minutes. That was a very nice trip to take.

Chapter 18

BUYING PROPERTY AND FUNDRAISING

—∞∞∞—

We were in Gardena for twelve years, and during that time we bought several pieces of property for the church. We bought a fourplex right to the west of the church. It brought in a lot of income and it was worth a considerable amount more when they sold it. We had bought it for $275,000 in 2000, and they later sold it (after we had left) for somewhere around $700,000! We had made it available for one of the missionaries that had moved to the area to work at Chi Alpha at UCLA. They stayed there about two years. We also bought a building next door for parking. We had the building torn down. Then we bought another building next to that one and had it torn down, too. We had increased the value of the property from $700,000 in '94 to over 3.5 million during those twelve years.

One of the things we had been wanting to do was to send our youths to youth camp, but we just did not seem to have the funds to do so. In 1999, the city voted to allow fireworks to be sold. They were going to have eight stands each year. They only made it available to non-profit groups. Then they were going to have a drawing to decide who would get these stands, and they could have them as long as they wanted them. Thirty-two groups put in the paperwork. They had the drawing at city hall. That place was packed. They started to draw the names and post them, and I was on the edge of my seat. We had the favor of God that day, because we were the fourth one drawn! We were the only church group to get one. We worked with Freedom Fireworks at that time, and they had gotten several locations. We told them we wanted a certain street corner. We had that location for about five years, but they went up so high on the price for that corner that we later moved to another location. That first year we sold about $68,000 worth of fireworks. Our part came to over $25,000. We made twice as much as any other group. With that money, we were able to send all the youths who wanted to go to camp. That had been one great fundraiser for the church and school.

While we were there, we supported as many as thirty-three missionaries per month. I believe that is what blesses a church, because, through that, you are ministering to the poor and those around the world that have not heard the Word of God.

During that time, we always had people come by who were in need. For many years we had a food bank, and we would give out food on Mondays. Many times we were able to help over a hundred families each month.

Chapter 19

MISSION TRIP

I feel I need to mention Larry Key again. We supported Larry Key as much as we did anyone else. Larry would come to the church for a weekend or three or four days, and we always had a great turnout. We connected him with several of the pastors in the area, and he would come to any size church. Larry was like a son to me. He would call me at different times, and we would talk for awhile. He was always welcome to stay at our house. In August of 2001, Larry invited Betty and I to go to the Philippines to help with a week of ministering to the pastors. Larry had invited two other couples to go as well. We left on a Sunday night and arrived there on Tuesday morning. It was a seventeen-hour flight! We were blessed to be able to stay in Shangri La, the best hotel in Manila.

Larry had been blessed to arrange a very good rate for us. The manager was a Christian and had been to many of Larry's revivals that he held there.

I was blessed to be able to speak four times, and the last time I spoke, I told part of my story. Now you have to understand that in the Philippines, they do not expect a person who is blind to be able to do anything at all. They were so surprised when I got to speak and teach the Word of God. As I told my story, the pastors began to cry. By the time I got through talking about how God had used many men and women in the Bible, they could see that God would use anyone if they were willing. I had so many pastors come up to me and say they were so touched by the sermon that they were going back to start more churches. The pastor who was over other pastors stood up and talked about that sermon for an hour.

They had only a few minutes before we started the night service. What a service we had that night. Several people were healed and several were saved. The next day one of the main pastors came over and asked if he could have my notes on that sermon. I asked him how many pastors wanted a copy. He said every one of them wanted a copy. I heard that almost every one of them preached that sermon in their churches the next Sunday! I was so grateful.

On Saturday we were to go on an outing up to the falls. It was at least two hours out, depending on the traffic. You see, over there you can only drive every other day depending on your tag and whether it ended in even or odd numbers. Odd numbers drove on certain days, while even drove the other days. On Sunday everyone can drive, and it is a nightmare to get around. Anyway, the traffic was very heavy that day. There were five of us men in the back van, and the ladies were in the front van. Our driver thought he had to keep up with the one in front, because he did not know where he was going. So on several occasions, he took chances. The last time he tried to pass on a two-lane road while going at least sixty miles per hour, and there came a big bus. He was in the left lane and everyone in the vehicle was getting ready to hit the deck except for me, because I could not see what was happening. It was only by an act of God that we were able to squeak through unharmed. That was a really close call. They later told me it was a good thing that I could not see what was happening. The trip back was uneventful.

I was invited to preach at one of the churches in Manila the next Sunday. It was a very small church, had no air conditioning, and was at least 100 degrees with humidity at about 100 percent. I preached for about an hour and was wet from head to toe. I drank three bottles of water after I got through. They gave us a wonderful meal in a room by ourselves. The pastor sat and watched us and waited on us hand and foot. Eventually, I asked to go to the bathroom, and I was so surprised. It was just a hole in the ground, with no toilet paper whatsoever. There was a bucket of water. You can figure out what that was used for. I was later talking to one of the missionaries and found out that was the case all over that area. We are so blessed to live in a country like the USA!

I remember several trips that we took during my time in the Air Force. We spent some time in poor conditions, but most of the time we had running water and restrooms. While we were in Vietnam, they still had not put in hot water by the time I left in January 1967.

On Larry's last trip to the Philippines, the doctor had told him he needed to stay at the hospital in order to get his blood pressure down. He was having pains in his chest. The doctor at the hospital told him he could die on the plane if he went. He was to have meetings in the Philippines, and he had promised them that he would be there. So he went anyway. They said Larry was having pain on the way there, and when they got about three hours out of the Philippines, he had a massive heart attack. They could not bring him back. They called me sometime that day, and I just broke down and cried. I really felt I had lost a son. They had four memorial services for him. One was in St. Louis, Missouri. It was packed. We also had a memorial service in Phoenix, Arizona, and I did that service. They had one for him in Mexico and also had one in the Philippines. The churches in the Philippines bought him the most expensive casket. It looked like gold. It took some time to get the body back to the states. They flew it back to the states and then into Chicago and were supposed to fly it to St. Louis, but the plane was too small for the casket, so the funeral home drove three hundred miles to get the casket. The crazy thing was that an ice storm came all that night, and the driver was not able to travel very fast. He made it back with only an hour to spare before the funeral was to start. Larry Key had been a blessing to many people across this nation and around the world.

One thing we must do in the ministry is take care of our health. It is hard, in many ways, when you feel the call to follow Christ. I feel if Larry had taken care and stayed in the hospital and gotten his blood pressure under control, he might still be working for God down here. I heard this one time at a funeral: "His work is finished on this earth."

Chapter 20

DEALING WITH BLINDNESS

—⬯⬯⬯—

As I have already indicated several times, dealing with going totally blind over the years has been a challenge. Experiencing things like not being able to see stars at night to running over things at night has been frustrating. Then it was awful having people wondering if I was drunk or something. I remember several times, even in the office, when I would run into the wall or door and I could hear people snickering, "I wonder if he has been drinking today." There was one day I came out of my office and was going down the sidewalk when a child ran right into me and she got knocked down really hard. I really thought she was hurt pretty bad, but she was fine. There was another time when I was about ten years old. I was following my cousin out in the field and we were running really fast. All of a sudden I fell into a ditch that was about six feet deep, and I started yelling. My cousin couldn't find me at first, because he had seen the ditch and automatically jumped over it. But I was not able to see it. It had just rained a few days before, and you can imagine how dirty I must have been.

The amazing thing is that while I worked on live aircraft for eleven years, working days and nights, I never had an accident. We always wore helmets to protect our heads. I got a lot of cuts in those helmets, but I never walked off the wing or fell down the stairs. When I was in El Cajon, California, I went to a meeting, and I was following one of the principals in a church building. She turned and went down a stairwell. It was very dark, and I thought she had just turned a corner, but she actually went down. I did not see the stairs and fell down and sprained my ankle. Boy I was upset, because I thought I had broken it. To this day, I still have a lot of trouble with it. I think there is a bone chip in there somewhere.

I remember several times I would try and play basketball. I would tell them to throw me the ball, and it seemed that they would just hit me right in the face. I tried playing baseball, and I was good at it until we would play a night game. I could not pick up the ball. The coach would yell at me and say, "Did you see that ball?" Of course I could not see the ball at night! All that time, I thought I was normal.

Chapter 21

WHAT EXCUSE IS THERE?

———⊸∞⊷———

What I am trying to impart is that it doesn't matter what has happened to you. It is just a stepping stone for next level of challenges. Don't get mad at God, saying, "Oh me, why me?" If God did not think that you could bear what you are going through right now, He would not make you go through these challenges. You can do it.

I like the story of our President Roosevelt the day after Pearl Harbor was bombed. He was sitting around looking at all of his cabinet members who were looking down and very discouraged over what had just happened. He was sitting in his wheelchair and he began to stand up on his very weak legs that had braces. Finally, he came to a standing position while everyone is wondering what he was going to do. He began to speak. The words that come out of his mouth caused them to react with amazing results. He said, "If I can stand on these legs, you can stand up and take charge and go get those bastards. Now get out of here, and let's go get them." That changed their whole attitude, and you know the rest of the story.

Look at Helen Keller, someone who could not hear or see, and we all know what she did.

It is all about your attitude in how you are going to react to the problems you are dealing with. They are really not problems. They are just challenges that we need to overcome. You can sit around and feel sorry for yourself or you can, get up and do something about it. Don't just sit there. Get up now.

Chapter 22

IN OUR WEAKNESS, HE IS STRONG

God used many people, none of whom were perfect. We can start with Abraham, who was a liar. He told a king that Sarah was his sister, which was true, she was his half-sister. But she was also his wife. God did not cut him off because of that mistake. He promised him that he would have descendants like the stars and the sands of the sea. He promised him a child in his old age, and God gave him one even though his wife was past the child-bearing age. So what is the real answer in this story? It is that God is not through with you yet, no matter what you have done.

Look at Jacob. That guy was a deceiver. He stole the birthright and blessing from his brother.

He pretended to be his brother, Esau, when Isaac was about to die. His mother even helped him take goat hair and put it on his arms and put his brother's clothes on so that he would smell like Esau. Jacob received the firstborn blessing and then ran for his life, because he knew his brother would be very upset with him. He ran to his uncle, who then deceived Jacob by giving him Leah instead of Rachel, whom he wanted. Then his uncle changed his wages ten times during the twenty years he was with him. Even a deceiver can become something for God. Rise up, old deceiver, and ask forgiveness from God! Then forgive yourself.

Joseph was a dreamer, and that got him thrown into a well then sold as a slave. While a slave in Egypt, he started doing well, until his boss's wife falsely accused him. That got him thrown into jail, where he again did so well that he was placed in charge of taking care of all the prisoners. During that time, two of Pharaoh's officials fell out of favor, got thrown into the same jail as Joseph, and then had dreams which Joseph was able to interpret. When the cupbearer's dream of being reinstated into Pharaoh's favor came to pass, Joseph asked him to remember him. But he forgot until two years later, when Pharaoh had a dream that no one could interpret. The cupbearer finally remembered Joseph and told Pharaoh about his ability. Pharaoh commanded that Joseph be brought to him.

God not only gave Joseph the ability to interpret the dream, but He gave him favor with Pharaoh. He saw great wisdom in Joseph and promoted him to second-in-command. Joseph was able to collect and save tons and tons of grain during the seven years of plenty, before the seven years of famine that were about to come on all the land. From slave to jailbird to second-in-command—what a promotion! Just because you have done things wrong, made mistakes, or even gotten thrown into jail, it's not too late. You can still do something great and make a difference.

I know a guy who was working on Wall Street and taking care of big hedge funds. He got caught doing something illegal and had to go to jail for several years. He asked God to help him while he was in prison, and God protected him from the biggest and meanest inmate. He was able to get out in a few short years, and during that time God had called him to be a missionary. He went to Mexico to minister down there, where he met his new wife. You see, before, because of what had occurred, he had lost his whole family. So God is able to bring us out.

So I ask this question again. "What is your challenge?" Think about all the people in wheelchairs and the things they do. You can do it!

You are created in God's image. You are armed and dangerous with the weapons he has given you: the breastplate of righteousness, the belt of truth, the helmet of salvation, the shoes of peace, the shield of faith, the sword of the Spirit. You have to remember that no weapon formed against you shall prosper. We have to look at the beginning of John 14:1, "Do not let your hearts be troubled ...." (NIV)

Don't forget, we are created for His pleasure. You have a destiny no matter who you are, what you look like, or what disability you have. We have to stand on the promise in Romans 8:28, "And we know that in all things God works for the good of those who love Him ...." (NIV)

We all need to get over the fear of failure. Those who never make mistakes do nothing. Jesus was the only one who did not make mistakes. God made you just like you are.

Genesis 25–37 talks about the story of Jacob. God uses imperfect people. Look at Jacob, a liar and deceiver. He stole his brother's birthright and blessing. He ran away to some of his kinfolk and worked twenty years for his uncle, who also deceived him. But one night on his way back to his homeland, he had an encounter with an Angel of the Lord, and from that time on he was a changed man. God changed his name to Israel, but when he was written about in the New Testament, he was called Jacob. That is to remind us that he was not perfect, and God still used him to create David and even Jesus.

Let us look at Moses. He was a killer. He killed one of the Egyptians who was harassing one of the Hebrews. The next day he saw two Hebrews fighting and tried to intervene. The one asked Moses if he was going to kill him too. He knew he was in trouble and ran away to the backside of the desert for forty years.

One day he saw the bush on fire that was not burning up and had to see what was causing of that. When he got close to it, God began to speak to him, telling him to take off his shoes because he was standing on holy ground. Taking off your shoes in the hot desert certainly is not a good idea, because that sand gets very hot. But Moses obeyed and went closer, and God began to tell him that he was to go back to Egypt and bring out the Hebrews who had been enslaved for over four hundred years after Joseph died. Then Moses began to make excuses, like he was slow to speak and could not do it. God told him that He would send his brother to find him and then help him by speaking for him. When they got in front of Pharaoh, something came over Moses, and he began to speak with a boldness he never knew he had.

That is what God has done for me. Many times I have gotten up to speak and did not know what I was going to say, but something would come over me. My mouth would open and God would speak through me, and it would be the message that the people needed to hear.

Joshua 2 begins the story of Rahab. She is a very interesting person in the battle of Jericho. Joshua sent two spies to scope out Jericho. While there, they had been spotted. They were taken into the house of Rahab, a prostitute. She sheltered them from the authorities and helped them escape, undetected, through her window. She had told them that she heard about what the Hebrew's God had done for them. She believed in their God and was willing to do all she could to help. She asked if they would spare her and her family, and they gave her instructions to follow so that her whole family would be saved when they came back to destroy Jericho. The story does not end there. She is saved, gets married to one of the Hebrews, and ends up being one of the great-grand-mothers of David himself! Not only that, but she is listed in the lineage of Jesus.

Now let's look at David and the things he had done. He committed several serious sins, including adultery and murder. He repented and was called a man after God's own heart. Why? For one thing, he repented of his sin. That is the key for all of us. If we do something wrong, we have to repent and make it right.

Peter was a hothead. Several times Jesus had to put him in his place. But after the day of Pentecost, Peter was a changed man. Paul was a killer, but he had a real turnaround. He was blinded by God and then was healed and became a Christ follower. He became the first missionary. Plus, he wrote half of the New Testament.

Chapter 23

ODDS AND ENDS

———⟨⟨⟩⟩———

Here are a few short stories some of you may like.

One time some of my cousins were over and we found a water hole out in the field that had about three feet of water in it. It had rained the night before and it was very hot, so we decided to go swimming, clothes and all. We were having a great time, and then that water began to get really muddy. We started getting hungry, so we headed back to the house. Mom saw us coming in the door and she told us we were not coming in like that. We were dirty from head to foot, with mud all over our clothes. She took us outside and took the water hose, turned the water on us, and washed all the mud off us. Then we had to sit on the porch until we dried off some before we could come in to eat. We did not do that again.

Another time I was about fourteen years old, and dad told me to change the oil in the car. He told me to just unscrew the plug on the bottom of the engine and let the oil out. So I got under the car, found the plug, unscrewed it, let the oil out, and put the plug back on. Then I put the oil in the engine. Well, Dad got home and I said to him, "Dad, you know, that oil sure was black." Dad knew something was wrong, so he lifted the hood and checked the oil level and got really mad. He said, "Do you know what you did? You drained the transmission grease out and added the new oil on top of the old oil!" Well, we had to drive it over to town and put it on the lift and put grease back in and drain half the oil out. He showed me where the oil plug was on the engine, and I never again drained the transmission. That was one lesson learned.

Another time we had a flat tire on the pickup, so dad had to drive the car to work. He left instructions for me to change the tire and get it fixed. Well, I was able to jack up the front and began to take the wheel nuts off. While doing so, I began to get ants on me. I got the tire changed and ran in the house crying that

I had ants all over me. Mom put me in a tub of hot water after I took all my clothes off. Please note you should not use hot water in a case like this. But Mom did not know any better at the time. We got all the ants off, but about then I began to have a reaction and started swelling up all over from all the bites. She called the hospital and they told her to get me to the ER as fast as she could. By the time I got there, I was going into shock. They gave me a shot of something, and in about thirty minutes I started coming out of it. I do not know how many times those ants bit me. I still do not like ants.

When I was about seven years old, my sister and I kept asking Dad if we could ride the horse. He finally gave in and put the saddle on the horse and put us in the saddle. Well, all was fine until we got about a half mile down in the field, where that horse decided it could do whatever it wanted. So, all of a sudden, it turned around and started running like crazy back to the house. I was pulling on the reins, but she would not stop. That horse was used to someone that was strong. Dad heard us fly by. We were both crying, because we were just hanging on. Needless to say, I did not ask to ride that horse again 'til I got much older.

One time my sister had a red dress on and was in the cow pen for something, and our bull saw her and that red dress. He started at her and she ran like crazy to get out of that pen. That bull did not like red at all.

We used to have some geese, and we had one old male goose. Every time I would go outside around where he was, he would start to charge after me. One day I picked up a rock and I threw it as hard as I could and hit him right in the head. He went down, and I thought I killed him. I must have been about seven at that time, and I came running in the house saying I had killed that goose. Dad went running out to see for sure. About that time, that goose started getting up and walking around, trying to see what happened. You know, he never ran after me anymore after that.

Chapter 24

CLOSING:
NO EXCUSES

———⊗⊗⊗———

To close out this book, I am going to use the story found in Luke 14. A certain man had prepared a feast. He told his servants to go and tell everyone that he had invited to come and that everything was ready. The first one said he had just bought some land and had to go and check it out. Who goes out and buys a house without looking at it except an investor? Maybe that was what he was. But he asked to be excused.

The next person had bought some oxen and had to go and try them out. Now who goes out and buys a car without driving it first? I guess I have bought some at auction without driving them. But anyway, he also asked to be excused. The next man to be invited said that he just got married and could not make it either. The host was so upset that he told his servants to go out and get those on the highways and byways and bring them in. The servants told their lord that there was still room. So he told them to go get the lame and sick and all the poor and compel them to come in so that his house may be filled. This story in the Bible is very interesting to me, because Jesus is telling us that we have no excuses. This is the primary thought I am trying to get to get across to each of my readers. It does not matter who you are. You have a destiny.

Yes, I am totally blind now, cannot hear out of one ear, and the other ear has a 50 percent loss. Plus, I have a number of other things that have affected me from the Vietnam War. But I am so blessed to have a wonderful wife, two boys, and eight grandchildren who have helped me. As of this writing, I still get to preach several times a month, and we have a care group of seniors (people over fifty) that meets at our house at least once a month. The title of this book is *I'm Blind. What's Your Excuse?* What I am trying to say is that we have no excuse. We all are God's handiwork, and each one of us has destiny.

So stop making all those excuses and get out and do something! If you cannot get out, become a prayer warrior for God. That is what America needs right now more than anything—some prayer warriors who can come boldly to the throne of grace and really pray.

Thanks for taking time to read this book.

Dr. Ron Lester

D r. Lester "has sermon, will travel." Please contact him today if he can encourage you by speaking at your church, retreat, or special event.

Website: www.drronlester.com

E-mail: ronlester45@gmail.com

Phone: 520-741-1217

CPSIA information can be obtained
at www.ICGtesting.com
Printed in the USA
FSHW02n1908300618
50013FS